RELEASED

THE PERIPHERAL WORKER

THE
PERIPHERAL WORKER

DEAN MORSE

NEW YORK AND LONDON
COLUMBIA UNIVERSITY PRESS
1969

This report was prepared for the Manpower Administration, U.S. Department of Labor, under research contract Numbers 26231-26244 authorized by Title I of the Manpower Development and Training Act. Since contractors performing research under government sponsorship are encouraged to express their own judgment freely, the report does not necessarily represent the department's official opinion or policy. Moreover, the contractor is solely responsible for the factual accuracy of all material developed in the report.

Reproduction in whole or in part permitted for any purpose of the United States government.

FOREWORD

by ELI GINZBERG

THERE IS a paradox built into modern scholarship. The concepts and approaches that receive attention and are worked on year after year by multiple investigators are inevitably improved and refined. In the process they attract more and more of the available scientific capital. The counterpoint of this trend is the substantial or total neglect of other areas which are not in fashion, in which the theoretical apparatus is relatively primitive and for which the data have not even been gathered.

It is a venturesome man who is willing to move against the trend. Dean Morse's *The Peripheral Worker* is the product of such an investigator—one who does not shy away from plunging into a difficult subject even though he must proceed with an ax rather than a scalpel, who must restrict himself to analyzing relatively gross data, and who knows before he starts that he will not be able to do much more than map the field.

In the 1930s, as a result of the urgency of the times, a framework was developed in the United States and in West European countries for systematically analyzing the participation of the adult population in the world of work. With unemployment rampant and persistent, with underemployment prevalent, with persons so discouraged that they ceased looking for jobs, information about, and analysis of, the labor force was pushed aggressively in order to achieve greater understanding of economic developments and to help in shaping public policy, particularly with respect to unemployment. By the end of World War II many of the conceptual and statistical difficulties involved in this new effort had been ironed out. Since 1947, we in the United States have had more or less consistent data about key aspects of American labor force behavior. There is no figure in the public domain, including the Federal Reserve index of industrial production and the Department of Commerce quarterly estimate of gross national product, that attracts more attention and concern than the release by the Departments of Commerce and Labor of the monthly rate of unemployment.

And yet this single figure hides almost as much as it discloses. If the population of the United States were sharply divided between workers and nonworkers—that is, people with jobs or looking for jobs and those who are outside the employment realm—such a single figure as the percentage of unemployed workers might have great meaning. But the patterns of labor force participation are much more complex—and it is toward illuminating this complexity that Professor Morse's book is directed. By drawing on the several disciplines of economics, sociology, and history he has sought to present and evaluate a more realistic model of the present structure of work and recent transformations of the ways in which different groups within the American population relate themselves to the world of work.

What does his term the "peripheral worker" connote? It refers to all the people who held a job at some time during the preceding year but who worked less than full time throughout the entire twelve months. It is a behavioristic concept: it simply defines as "peripheral" all who worked less than full time the full year. The concept makes no attempt to distinguish among those who are peripheral because they prefer to work less than full time, such as many married women and students; those who have entered the labor force at some time during the course of the year, such as those who have graduated from school; or those who have left it during the year for good and sufficient reasons, such as to have a baby. These constitute a second group whose peripherality is grounded in compelling alternatives.

The concept of peripherality as developed by Professor Morse is indeed broad: it includes many discrete subgroups. In addition to those who prefer to work less than full time, many change their roles from nonworker to worker or from worker to nonworker during the course of a year. A further peripheral group would prefer full-time work but cannot find it.

The concept of peripherality is so elastic as to warn against its uncritical use in explaining many aspects of labor force behavior. But the fact that a concept must be handled with care does not imply that it is irrelevant or wrong. The striking point around which Professor Morse conducts his analysis is the fact that approximately 45 percent of all Americans who had work in one year fall within the category of "peripheral" workers. While this statistic has been in the public realm ever since the Department of Labor began to publish its data on "work experience," circa 1950, the phenomenon has not attracted the attention of students.

Three potent forces are intricately related to this phenomenon. The first reflects the ever larger role played by women, particularly married women, in the American economy. One need only recall that, prior to World War II, when a woman married she was frequently forced to resign her job. Today most women who work—and women account for approximately a third of the labor force—are married. And most married women, especially those with children at home, prefer to work less than full time the full year.

A second explanation of the high proportion of peripheral workers in the total labor force is the vast expansion and elongation of our education and training. Today about three out of four young people remain in school long enough to obtain a high school diploma. About half of these graduates go on to junior college, a four-year college, or some other type of further schooling or training. Many remain in school until their early or even late twenties. Since the majority of students must meet part, if not all, of their expenses, they tend to combine study with work. They account for a second major group of peripheral workers. Once again we have a social transformation that dates from World War II—particularly with regard to the element of scale.

The third large subgroup of peripheral workers is composed of the disadvantaged, particularly those who are handicapped for employment because of poverty, location, race, or other stigmas. They are the workers who in the literature of yesterday were called "marginal" workers. They find themselves at the end of the queue when it comes to competing for jobs. Since the number of regular jobs available is smaller than the number of workers seeking them, those who are in the weakest competitive position have to accept what is left. Although they might prefer to work full time—and many would —they will have to accept what they can get. Many are forced to accept seasonal work. Others have no choice but to take jobs that offer only a few hours' rather than a full day's work. It should be noted in this connection that the number of persons unemployed during the course of a year is about three to four times the number unemployed at any one time. Several million suffer two or three or even more spells of unemployment during the course of one year.

Among the most interesting questions that Professor Morse

raises although he is unable to provide a definitive answer is the extent to which "peripherality" has changed over the last seventy or so years since the United States first became an industrialized country. He makes these points: at the turn of the century large numbers joined the urban labor force from the farm and from abroad. As he sees it, newcomers always confront multiple difficulties in becoming fully acclimated to their new surroundings and in becoming fully attached to their world of work. Hence peripherality is likely to be part of their life style until they sink deeper roots. Moreover, because they are yokels or greenhorns, they find themselves at the end of the queue. The better—more regular—jobs are preempted by those who have preferred status, those who have been longer established.

This suggests a partial parallelism between then and now because conspicuous among the large numbers of present-day peripheral workers are the young, females, and the disadvantaged—all groups of low status.

Professor Morse is not able to delineate fully the extent to which the changing industrial structure and the occupational mix have shifted the balance over the intervening period to expanding or contracting peripherality. He is willing to risk a judgment that on balance the transformation of the economy has tended to moderate the factors contributing to peripherality. This much is clear from his analysis. It would be foolish to hold on to a picture of the past in which all workers, or even most workers, started before sunrise and continued until sundown, six days a week. Many worked long weeks but few worked such a schedule for 52 weeks in the year.

In his analysis of peripheral work in our contemporary economy, Professor Morse makes clear that it is concentrated heavily in three sectors: agriculture, trade, and services. Manufacturing is substantially free of peripherality, as is government employment.

According to occupational categories, a similar heavy concentration is found. One out of three peripheral workers is a private household worker, retail salesman, farm worker, waiter, or general laborer. This tells us further that a high proportion of peripheral workers is engaged in work requiring little skill and earns low wages.

It is this latter point which leads Professor Morse to raise the disturbing question of whether and to what extent the American labor force is becoming bifurcated. As he sees it, one part of the labor force consists of those whose employment is full time the full year with important fringe benefits. It includes those who obtain employment with large, responsible employers who are able to create and maintain good working conditions. The other group is composed of the large number of workers who cannot gain a toehold in the preferred sector of the economy and must accept employment where they can find it, usually with small employers in the services or trades where wages are low, fringe benefits are few or nonexistent, and work is part time and/or intermittent. The recent book published by Professor Morse's colleague, Dr. Marcia Freedman, on *The Process of Work Establishment* (New York: Columbia University Press, 1969), surely lends support to this hypothesis.

But even if there is a bifurcation, we must quickly add that peripherality is not all bad. In fact, it makes it possible for many women, students, and some of the disadvantaged, such as older persons, to have some work experience during the year. If confronted with the alternative of working full time or not at all, many would have to opt reluctantly for the latter. Moreover, part-time, part-year employment is a boon to many employers because it provides the flexibility to respond to fluctuating demands in the market without steady high costs. To this extent, peripheral work contributes to ensuring adequate supplies at reasonable prices to the consumer.

What, then, are the critical policy issues to which an ever more affluent society should be alert and responsive?

Several million persons currently report themselves as working less than full time during the course of a year for "economic reasons," which is a euphemism for their inability to find a full-time job. Hence one major objective of public policy should be to strive to establish and maintain as high a level of employment as possible, short of generating inflationary pressures.

The fact is that many women who now work part time would welcome an opportunity to work full time if they could make other arrangements for discharging their responsibilities at home, particularly child care. Congress has slowly come to realize that inadequate child care facilities are particularly burdensome on the poor and near-poor. Many mothers desire to work, or would prefer to work full time rather than part time, but they can do so only if their children can be properly supervised. Here is another area where sound public policy could have constructive results.

Many young people need some experience in the world of work while they are still in school and others need opportunities to work to help support themselves while in school. Peripheral work opportunities in larger number than are currently available are required for these young people—more work-study programs and more summer employment. In both areas, the economy has been characterized by a serious shortfall. It may well be that if there are inherent limitations which prevent the substantial expansion of such opportunities in the private sector, much more should be done by government in the public sector.

To the extent that Professor Morse's theories about low status migrants and peripherality have validity—and I feel that they do—more should be done to improve the quantity and quality of labor market services to those who contemplate relocation as well as for those who have recently relocated. Additional support for these workers may go a long way to reducing the period during which they are forced to remain on the periphery of the economy, fluctuating between work and relief.

A more difficult challenge, but one that should no longer be ignored, is how a civilized and affluent society can provide appropriate work opportunities for millions of older persons who retire in their early or middle sixties. It is not only wasteful but cruel to assign them to the scrapheap of the unwanted. Many are able and want to continue to work— if not full time, then part time. We need to face up to this challenge and opportunity.

Finally, we dare not assume that because so many women are currently employed our society has solved the problem of womanpower. It has not. A major and continuing challenge is to devise new ways of creating opportunities for many millions of able women who desire to work part time part of the year for whom there are no jobs—surely no jobs commensurate with their abilities and potential. Here is another possible resource that warrants public attention and action.

Professor Morse's work on peripherality has helped to throw new and penetrating light onto the employment problems facing the disadvantaged, youth, older persons, and women. If the work of a social scientist is assessed in terms of its contribution to knowledge and to public policy, then Professor Morse must be congratulated on meeting both criteria.

PREFACE

AT ITS INCEPTION this study was conceived to be a modest monograph on a subject suggested by the Director of the Conservation of Human Resources Project of Columbia University, Dr. Eli Ginzberg. His suggestion was agreeable to me for several reasons. I had never been engaged in formal or active work in problems involving labor and human resources and felt that the study would give me an opportunity to explore some questions I had long been interested in. But I was primarily drawn to the investigation because it seemed to me that it was possible that the problems of the individuals and social groups whose relationship to the labor market placed them in what we initially decided to call the "peripheral labor force" might be related to a host of other social problems, many of them of increasing importance and severity.

But there was another explanation for my acceptance of Dr. Ginzberg's proposal. Perhaps the gentlest term to ascribe to it is "innocence." I had at the outset little conception of the complexity of the subject, little awareness of the demands which a thorough investigation would make upon a would be investigator's theoretical, statistical, and practical sophistication. Increasing awareness of such demands, however, does not automatically increase competence.

The only sensible solution to this intellectual "technological gap," a kind of nonsolution in fact, was, it seemed to me, to keep away from some of the difficult and challenging problems that an economist might be expected to tackle, particularly the creation and testing of a model whose variables would provide at least a partial explanation of why it is that certain demographic groups or types of individuals tend to be attached to the labor market less strongly than others. Some of the variables that might go into such a model suggest themselves immediately: wage rates, job search costs, other opportunity costs, education, training, location, family status, age, sex, and color.

There were other reasons for not attempting to carry out that kind of investigation. On the one hand, it seemed to me that wage data for the parts of the working population that I had primarily in mind were necessarily somewhat incomplete. A more important reason, however, was my feeling that a satisfactory model would have to incorporate longitudinal data which at present are not available in sufficient detail. Indeed, the absence of comprehensive data on the entire working lives of those demographic groups upon whom this study concentrates is a very serious handicap. The basic statistical data of much of the study come from the surveys of work experience conducted once a year for the Bureau of Labor Statistics. They represent a snapshot of the problem where in many ways it would be very desirable to have a moving picture instead. Our data, for example, cannot help but include among those we have called peripheral workers a number of adult workers whose total work history is not really peripheral at all.

Finally, I decided at the outset not to take up the thorny problem of voluntary and involuntary peripheral work experience. Certainly much of peripheral work experience as we have defined it is voluntary in any sense of the term. At the same time, I felt that the responses to the questions in the annual survey of work experience designed to throw light on why people work part time could not always help us to determine why a person's total working life came to be peripheral. It seems possible that in a significant number of cases certain demographic groups become so accustomed to certain kinds of peripheral work experience that they come to feel that their acceptance of this kind of work experience is entirely voluntary. For example, women who work part of the year in food canning plants in areas where other opportunities for industrial work are very limited during the rest of the year come to think that the pattern of their work experience is voluntary when, in fact, the establishment in their neighborhood of opportunities for full-year work of a similar character could induce an increasing fraction of this group to work a longer part of the year.

So much for what the author knows to be several shortcomings and gaps in his way of approaching the problem. There are undoubtedly other defects of which he is less conscious, but for which he bears complete responsibility. Whatever merits the study may have he feels much less responsible for. He has been the grateful recipient of counsel and help from many people and the following acknowledgments cannot really do justice to the patience and generosity of those who read part or all of the manuscript in its various stages of completion, discussed knotty questions, and made enlightening suggestions of substance and form, fact and hypothesis. My primary debt is to the Director of the Conservation of Human Resources Project of Columbia University, without whose guidance and encouragement the study could not have been made.

A number of those on the staff of the Conservation of Human Resources Project provided helpful comment and criticism, but I hope that those who are not mentioned by name will forgive me if I single out Marcia Freedman, Ivar Berg, Alfred Eichner, Stanley Friedlander, Harry Greenfield,

Dale Hiestand, and Beatrice Reubens, each of whom made valuable suggestions. The first listed of these colleagues was unfailingly helpful at all stages of the investigation and she alone knows the debt I owe her for her assistance. Arnold Katz of the University of Pittsburgh supervised the cross-tabulation of a number of variables from the 1960 1-1000 census tapes, which helped me immensely. In addition he read the completed manuscript and provided me with invaluable and detailed criticism. I regret that my own incapacities prevented me from using some of his more important critical comments more fruitfully. He knows, I hope, how much I am aware that the study lacks the kind of theoretical and empirical substance which he would have liked to see in it. Moses Abramowitz of Stanford University was kind enough to read the manuscript and to make a number of very helpful comments.

I owe, finally, a great debt to Chryss Lieberfreund and Sylvia Leef of the administrative staff of the Conservation of Human Resources Project for their many kindnesses. Eva Gilleran typed many drafts of the manuscript with unfailing accuracy and good humor for which I am very grateful. Mr. William Bernhardt of the Columbia University Press provided me with most expert and understanding editorial supervision.

A substantial portion of Chapter VII of this book first appeared in Eli Ginzberg and Associates, *Manpower Strategy for the Metropolis* (New York: Columbia University Press, 1968). Portions of Chapter IV appeared in an altered form under the title "The Peripheral Worker in the Affluent Society," in the Proceedings of the 20th Annual Winter Meeting, 1968, of the Industrial Relations Research Association.

Columbia University   DEAN MORSE
January, 1969

CONTENTS

THE PERIPHERAL WORKER

⊰ CHAPTER I ⊱
THE PROBLEM AND
ITS SETTING

FEW QUESTIONS can be more important for modern society than the size and character of the labor force. An immense amount of statistical information is being collected which shows in considerable detail the composition of the American labor force. A number of increasingly sophisticated econometric studies have been carried out to pinpoint the variables which determine the participation of important demographic subgroups in that force.[1] Prophecies of rapid technological change and concomitant increases in labor productivity have led to heightened concern about the economy's ability to employ the vast numbers who will enter the labor force in the next decades.

It is confidently asserted by some that the solution to this problem will be an increase in leisure and that the real problem is to make sure that this leisure is allocated as equitably as possible and to develop attitudes toward leisure which emphasize its constructive possibilities. According to this version of the future, a major irony of the emerging situation is that

[1] See Jacob Mincer, "Labor Force Participation and Unemployment, a Review of Recent Evidence," in Robert A. Gordon and Margaret S. Gordon, *Prosperity and Unemployment* (New York: John Wiley and Sons, 1966), pp. 73–112, for a critical examination of some of these studies.

those who can least use leisure (the uneducated, the unskilled, the low-paid) will be the unwilling beneficiaries of society's capacity to create unprecedented amounts of leisure, while the very group most able to value leisure and to use it properly (the well educated, the rich, and the resourceful) will be driven by the needs of new technology to work longer and harder.

While statisticians and econometricians are providing ever more complete and sophisticated data and statistical analyses of the changing dimensions of the labor force, other developments, occurring within the domain of economic theory proper, have stirred interest in the question of the composition of that force. Basically these theoretical developments have resulted from, among other things, a thoroughgoing effort to extend the elements of economic theory to nonmarket activities of individuals. The developments emphasize the importance of a careful consideration of opportunity costs when, for example, educational activity is being analyzed or when women shift their activity from home to the market place.[2]

At the same time these theoretical developments ask searching questions about how an individual allocates time. The shape of lifetime earnings profiles is being carefully investigated; such profiles necessarily call attention to an individual's work experience over a long sequence of years. It is being increasingly recognized, moreover, that changes in the relative prices of goods and services can have quite complicated effects upon an individual faced with the problem of allocating his time.

Against this background of widespread social concern about the distribution of work and leisure and the specific interests of economists in the theoretical issues involved, it is instructive to place traditional views of the formation of an industrial

[2] See Gary Becker, "A Theory of the Allocation of Time," *Economic Journal*, September, 1965, pp. 493–516.

labor force, paying particular attention to what these views have to say about work and leisure.

TIME, WORK, AND LEISURE:
THE FORMATION OF THE LABOR FORCE

One of the central problems investigated by economic historians writing of the past few centuries is the formation of a disciplined and stable labor force in the advanced economies of Western Europe. The usual model of the development of the labor force has been starkly simple. It is the story of the transformation of a predominantly agricultural work force whose life style was formed by the demands of a simple agricultural technology and the seasons. Hours of work, in this model, were determined largely by the diurnal round of the sun; days worked during the year were largely the result of the demands of planting and harvesting. The clock was unknown. Time was concrete, variable, and organic rather than abstract, fixed, and artificial.

With the coming of industrialism, the labor force became tied to the demands of a mechanical universe. No longer part of an organic society, the laborer could survive only by offering himself in the labor market and accepting the impersonal allocation of labor which that market imposed. A constant tendency of population to increase and the resulting tendency of the supply of labor to outstrip demand forced the laborer to accept subsistence wages and to work long hours. The large aggregations of capital that were necessary for the new industrialism put the employer under pressure to offer work to the laborer only if he was willing to accept long hours. The working day therefore began to extend beyond the bounds set by available sunlight; the factory bell or steam whistle, a collective alarm clock, made its appearance. Time became as mechanical as the new processes of production. The stream of laborers—father, mother, and children—flowed into the factory in the early morning hours. At night, after a work day which frequently stretched past twelve hours, they trudged homeward to find temporary rest.

But there was no respite the next morning, for, according to this version of the history of the laboring classes, industrialism, which freed the process of production from its daily organic time, was just as effective in freeing man from the seasonal forces which structured his activity in more primitive ages. His freedom, however, was illusory. The mechanical processes of production could operate the year round. The work year therefore began to approximate the calendar year, the only interruption of work being the weekly Sabbath, a vestige of a more flexible past which resisted, because of its sacred character, the encroachments of the new mechanical universe of production.

In its final implications, the model asserts that the labor force tends to work, under the new industrialism, as many hours a day as the laborer can physically tolerate and as many days a year as a decaying system of religious holidays will tolerate. And to complete the model, there is the implicit assertion, to become explicit in the version offered by Marx, that the laboring class makes up a large, and increasing, proportion of the population.

The initial outcome of the process of transformation of the old agricultural labor force into the new industrial labor force is, in this traditional view, the division of society into two parts. On the one side there are proprietors and landlords, assisted by a relatively small professional contingent; on the other side there is the industrial labor force working long hours day after day, except for periods of economic crisis. The agricultural labor force that survives is considered to be simply a vestige of the past, and it is easily assumed that the work experience of the agriculturalist, now transformed into the agricultural day laborer, is roughly parallel to that of the industrial day laborer.

The usual view of the formation of the modern industrial labor force as it tends to appear in its simplest form has been sketched here because it seems to be so intimately related to our attitudes toward the work experience of the modern labor force as a whole and particularly to the question of the "peripheral worker" in contemporary American life.

THE PERIPHERAL WORKER:
A TENTATIVE DEFINITION

What, in fact, do we mean by the term "peripheral worker"? It would seem worth while at this stage of the investigation to take a rather general look at our "peripheral population." Those workers who are covered by the term "peripheral labor force" are, for the most part, those individuals who have had work experience of any kind other than full time for a full year. According to Special Labor Force Report No. 76, *Work Experience of the Population in 1965*, a very large number of people are included in this concept of the "peripheral labor force," some 38 million in that year. The total number of individuals who had any kind of work experience was slightly more than 86 million: some 48 million of these worked the full year at full-time jobs.[3] In subsequent pages the term "peripheral labor force" will be used to refer to the entire population of peripheral workers.

The reader should keep in mind that the "peripheral labor force" is *not* simply a portion of the labor force as defined by the Census Bureau. Its frame of reference is rather the work experience concept.

The severity of the impact of peripherality is variable. Peripherality does not constitute a problem for many of the

[3] Full-year work includes paid vacations.

individuals who are covered by the term "peripheral labor force." Rather it should be seen for them as the solution to what would otherwise be a problem. The variable work schedules and the freedom of entry and exit from the labor force which are involved in peripherality permit many individuals to participate in the world of work who might otherwise not be able to work at all, making possible for a significant number of workers a closer tailoring of the marginal utility of income to the marginal disutility of effort. It should also be noted that the work arrangements associated with peripherality permit a significant number of workers, who are not peripheral at all, to hold multiple jobs, so that in many cases they work far more hours during the week than what is considered full time.

Even for those workers who would prefer either to work a larger number of hours or to have a more regular job, peripheral employment experience frequently does not represent something negative in their work history. For many it represents an improvement over the only alternative, no work at all; for some it is an important part of the process of increasing commitment to the world of work; for those who are in the process of detaching themselves from work it is a desirable way-station on the journey to retirement.

From the point of view of the productive process, peripheral work furnishes an important part of the mechanism by which necessary variations in labor inputs are brought about. There is some optimum degree of flexibility in the productive process, difficult as it may be to specify what this optimum is and what are the elements that combine to create it. Nevertheless the desirable flexibility is probably greater in amount than is often thought. Shifting tastes, shifting resources, technological change, cyclical movements, and economic growth all require some degree of over-all flexibility in the economy and in each productive unit. Each productive unit, moreover, strives to create a margin of flexibility in its production process in a world of uncertainty and risk.

There is one exception in these influences that tend to make for flexibility of output. From the point of view of the individual worker, flexibility of output can be an unmitigated evil in a number of ways. Workers can be expected, as they achieve status, organization, and power, whether direct economic power or indirect political power, to strive to minimize the variability of their own employment. To the extent that a group of workers belong to favored institutions (either firms or labor organizations, the latter broadly conceived), it may be possible for them to shift the burden of flexibility of labor inputs to less protected, less sheltered, and less cohesive groups among the work force.

The attainment of flexibility, in other words, is costly and the question remains: "Who shall, or who can be forced to, pay the cost?" Flexibility in the typical producing unit can be expected to have a quite noticeable cost. It may be possible for the firm to arrange its affairs so that flexibility is furnished by other units, the firm being so constructed and organized that its own output is kept relatively constant, therefore enabling it to use the optimum technology related to constant output. Firms are under constant pressure to find some method either to reduce the cost of flexibility or to shift it onto someone else.

This suggests the possibility that at least some part of those workers who work part time or intermittently are peculiarly at the mercy of those agencies, whether firms or labor organizations or governmental agencies, whose actions in the labor market have the effect of shifting the burden of the cost of flexibility from themselves onto those who have no other recourse. If this is so, we would expect to find that part-time and part-year workers are composed to a large extent of those segments of the labor force that have been historically, and for very profound reasons still are, the weakest and most poorly organized.

It is a matter of some economic importance and even greater social consequence whether the group of workers whose work experience is part time or intermittent is a growing fraction of the total number of individuals with work experience during the year. Just as important is the question of whether the individuals who compose the peripheral labor force tend to be drawn in disproportionate numbers from recognizable demographic subdivisions of the total society or whether such a tendency is developing. Is the labor force becoming increasingly bifurcated into the regular full-time, full-year labor force and a peripheral labor force, more or less subordinate in status, wage rates, and fringe benefits? Are the barriers to movement from the peripheral labor force to the regular full-time, full-year labor force increasingly difficult to surmount for particular elements of the peripheral labor force? Do such workers tend to cluster disproportionately in certain sectors of the economy? Do they tend to cluster in certain occupations? Does the secular change in educational attainment of the labor force as a whole place segments of the peripheral labor force at a disadvantage by confining them increasingly to sectors and occupations in which investment in training is markedly less than in those sectors and occupations where the typical employee is a regular full-time worker?

Fundamentally, then, the problem of the peripheral labor force can be posed by these questions: What have been the changes in recent years in the demand for and the supply of workers whose attachment to the labor force is less firm than that of the central nucleus of full-time, full-year workers? How well has the labor market adjusted to changes in supply and demand involving the peripheral labor force? Have certain elements of the peripheral labor force tended to become increasingly "noncompeting groups" in the labor force, subject to inferior conditions of work, inferior wages, and inferior status? Do such groups, if they exist, suffer the added disability of partial or entire exclusion from some of the governmental programs designed to protect and to stabilize the position of the individual worker?

In comparing the different types of peripheral workers with the regular full-time, full-year worker, it is important to discover whether there are important differences in their lifetime work experience. Do some or most peripheral workers get excluded from the various processes by which the regular full-time, full-year worker moves upward through a hierarchy of jobs? Is peripheral work experience typically a "dead end" affair?

What kind of answers we give to the questions listed above depends to a large extent upon what time perspective we have in view. It is necessary to see the peripheral labor force not as a recent development but rather as an inherent and important part of the total labor force in the past. By comparing the experience of the peripheral worker of the past with his counterpart today it is possible to suggest those aspects of the present-day peripheral labor force which should give most cause for concern and those aspects which may represent desirable developments. It is to the question of the peripheral worker in the past that we turn in Chapter II.

◄ CHAPTER II ►
THE HISTORICAL
BACKGROUND

THERE HAS BEEN a long tradition of concern about those groups of workers who are included under the rubric "the peripheral labor force." The "casual" worker, for example, was one of the focal points of Charles Booth's classic study of London working-class life in the last decades of the nineteenth century. Investigations of specific aspects of peripheral attachment to the labor force were carried out in the early years of the twentieth century. Usually such studies were the outcome of immediate problems which had developed among workers whose attachment to the labor force was irregular. A notable example is the collection of essays by Carleton Parker, published posthumously under the title *The Casual Laborer*.[1] These essays focus upon agricultural labor in California in the early decades of the twentieth century, particularly upon a spectacular episode of labor unrest, the Wheatland riots, but they are also concerned with the problems of the migratory worker in general to whose plight IWW agitation was calling attention.

The longshoreman, the migratory agricultural worker, and other groups whose work experience tends to be peripheral

[1] Carleton Parker, *The Casual Laborer and Other Essays* (New York: Harcourt, Brace, and Howe, 1920).

have been the subjects of past investigations. But until the relatively recent past, there have been few studies which have centered upon the entire population of peripheral workers as we have defined the term. The lack of over-all investigations of those workers whose work experience took the form either of part-time or intermittent work can be explained in part by the fact that few statistical data were collected on this subject, except for fragmentary studies, until the Great Depression focused attention upon the need for improved employment statistics. Beginning with the 1940 census, however, systematic efforts have been made to collect such data. In both the 1940 and 1950 censuses questions were asked about the number of hours worked during the census week by employed workers. In addition information was collected on the number of weeks worked during the previous year by all individuals who had any work experience. In 1941 the Current Population Survey began to collect data on hours worked each month and, since 1951, information about weeks worked. Since 1955 material has also been collected on reasons for part-time or less than full-year work.

Using these new sources of data, Gertrude Bancroft devoted a chapter of *The American Labor Force* to "trends in the part-time labor force." [2] In one important respect her frame of reference differs from that adopted in this study. She focuses upon those members of the labor force whose part-time or intermittent status is voluntary in character. As she put it, "the terms 'part-time workers' and 'part-time labor force' will be used to describe those workers who do not *usually* work or seek to work full time the year round. . . . In the part-time labor force are persons who usually worked part time or who chose to work only part of the year because of home or school responsibilities." [3] Our definition covers a somewhat broader

[2] Gertrude Bancroft, *The American Labor Force: Its Growth and Changing Composition* (New York: John Wiley and Sons, 1958).
[3] *Ibid.*, p. 89.

group since it includes all workers who are not members of the full-time, full-year category, putting provisionally to one side the question of whether such peripheral status is voluntary or not. Miss Bancroft's chapter on the part-time worker provides an invaluable analysis of the characteristics of voluntary part-time work experience in the mid-1950s and contains a number of suggestive leads to further developments.

At the outset it would be useful to gain some sense of the characteristics and dimensions of the peripheral labor force in the past. Although the lack of uniform statistical data makes difficult precise quantitative comparisons between part-time or intermittent employment experience before World War II and the present day, it is possible to arrive at a qualitative sense of the characteristics of peripheral work experience in earlier periods. To this end, attention has been concentrated on the employment experience and the characteristics of peripheral labor at the turn of the century from 1890 to 1910.

It is often assumed that among the important secular trends that have shaped our contemporary economic order is a pervasive and drastic reduction in the number of hours the average worker puts in each week (and, by implication, each year). Typical of such attitudes is the following statement:

Statistics on hours of work for the whole labor force have been available only since 1940, when they were first obtained in the population census, but *it is generally known that hours have been greatly shortened during the last half century*. It is estimated that average full-time weekly hours in manufacturing industries were reduced from 59 in 1899 to 40 in 1939. The reduction for all types of employment has probably been less, but still very substantial.[4]

These impressions are perfectly understandable. One of the major aspects of labor history in the nineteenth century was the agitation for shorter working hours. The struggle for the

---

[4] John Durand, *The Labor Force in the United States, 1890–1960* (New York: Social Science Research Council, 1948), p. 21. Italics added.

ten-hour day, the evidence presented before parliamentary committees in England and before industrial commissions in the United States in the nineteenth century about excessive hours spent in mill and mine, statements as late as the early decades of the twentieth century that steel mills, for example, could not be operated except on a twelve-hour day and a seven-day week, the common belief that farmers worked from sunup to sundown—all such diverse evidence explains easily enough the general impression that the very long average hours in the nineteenth century were followed by a secular decline extending to the present day. In *America's Needs and Resources* by Dewhurst and Associates, this decline begins in 1850 and continues more or less uninterruptedly until 1940. Indeed the decline is, according to Dewhurst, most rapid from 1900 to 1920. Over the entire period from 1850 to 1940 he estimates that nonagricultural hours of work have fallen from 66 hours to approximately 40 hours (see Fig. 1). Again our everyday impressions are reinforced by spectacular instances of the process of shortening of work weeks in selected industries and occupations in the last few decades, buttressed by statistical evidence accumulating in these same years about actual hours worked. All such evidence confirms this belief about the secular movement of average hours. In sum it maintains that very large decreases in the length of the working week took place during the past hundred or so years, decreases which were most rapid in the period from 1900 to 1920 (when the average work week is supposed to have decreased about ten hours. Since 1940 the decrease has been relatively slight, not more than one or two hours over the entire period from 1940 to the present (although the average work week increased some five or six hours during World War II).

Yet even in his statement about the secular trend in hours, Durand notes that there are grounds for caution. He points out that "statistics on hours of work for the whole labor force have been available only since 1940," a period in which decreases in working hours have been, with some spectacular exceptions, really quite moderate. Then what is the basis of his judgment about the general decrease in hours between 1899 and 1939? The answer, of course, is that his authority for the statement, Fabricant, is dealing not with actual hours worked but with scheduled hours, "full-time" hours. There is little question that there must have been over these decades some more or less definite relationship between "full-time" hours and "actual hours worked." There is, however, very little that can be said about what the actual relationship in the whole economy might have been, even though estimates can be made for specific manufacturing industries and firms.

That hours were long in the nineteenth century in particular industries and occupations is of course not at issue. But it is important to remember that the long hours that Fabricant and Durand primarily have in mind were worked by that segment of the labor force that worked full-time work weeks in manufacturing. And if we are interested in average work weeks over the course of the year, we must add that such long average weekly hours were worked solely by those who not only worked full-time weeks but also worked the full year. If the experience of those who were not full-time, full-year workers were added, the picture might change significantly.

But here again there is an understandable tendency to assume that this fraction—the "peripheral labor force"—has increased in size over the past decades. Certainly that is the impression conveyed by some of the recent projections of the labor force for the next decade or so. In their *Labor Force Projections for 1970-80* Sophia Cooper and Denis Johnston conclude that "since a considerable part of the projected increase of 24 million in the total labor force between 1964 and 1970 will consist of those groups—younger workers and adult women—among whom part-time work is prevalent, the num-

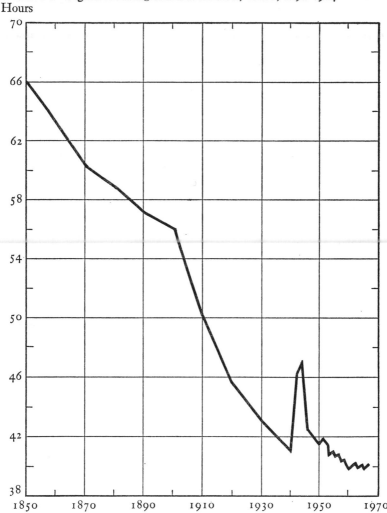

Figure 1. *Nonagricultural Hours of Work, 1850-1964*

NOTE: Data from 1943 to 1963 relate to actual hours of work during the survey week by members of the labor force who were at work. Data are for the month of May of each year and reflect hours worked at all jobs during the week. These figures are based on interviews obtained in the monthly survey of households.

SOURCES: 1850-1940; J. Frederic Dewhurst and Associates, *America's Needs and Resources* (New York: Twentieth Century Fund, 1955). 1943-1963: U.S. Bureau of the Census and U.S. Bureau of Labor Statistics.

ber of part-time workers will increase substantially." [5] More specifically related to the changes in the demographic composition of the labor force since World War II are the following statements to be found in another Special Labor Force Report in 1963:

Developments in the labor force and employment during the early 1960's largely represented a continuation of trends which have characterized the entire period since World War II. Adult women, many of whom choose to work part-time, continued to account for most of the growth in the labor force.[6]

Later in the same article the author states:

In addition, part-time working arrangements, so important to women with families, have become a common feature of the labor market. Voluntary part-time jobs appeared to be increasing as usual in the early 1960's, with virtually all the employment slowdown occurring among full-time workers.[7]

However, it should be noticed that the same article points out that two other demographic groups, teen-agers and older workers, whose labor force participation is relatively more part time in character than the central age males, have displayed decreasing labor force participation rates in the last few years, so it is not clear whether the author intends to give the impression that it is because of demographic changes that part-time employment is increasing in proportion to total employment experience.

Moreover, developments occurring in the years since 1960 clearly indicate that in point of fact the segment of the labor force that works full time the full year has very recently begun to account for a larger proportion of the total labor

[5] Special Labor Force Report No. 49, *Labor Force Projections for 1970–80* (Washington, D.C.: U.S. Department of Labor, Bureau of Labor Statistics), p. 130.

[6] Special Labor Force Report No. 31, *Labor Force and Employment, 1960–1962* (Washington, D.C.: U.S. Department of Labor, Bureau of Labor Statistics), p. 497.

[7] *Ibid.*, p. 501.

force. According to a Special Labor Force Report, "Approximately 55 percent . . . of those who worked in 1963 (about 45.4 million persons) worked full time for the whole year, the highest proportion since 1957. The 1.4 million rise over the year was the largest gain since 1955." [8] During 1964 the proportion of full-time, full-year workers rose slightly and the absolute number approached 47 million. By 1965 slightly more than 56 percent of the population with work experience during the year worked full time the entire year. (The exclusion of 14- and 15-year-old workers from the work experience survey in 1966 makes that year's proportion of full-time workers not comparable with earlier years.)

It would seem, therefore, that there is clear-cut evidence, at least for the period since the early 1960s, that full-time, full-year employment is accounting for a slightly larger share of total employment experience. This period, of course, is unusual in that it has also been the longest recorded period of uninterrupted expansion of the economy and a period in which unemployment rates slowly tended to decrease for almost all segments of the labor force. Unemployment rates for the central white male age groups, particularly for the married, have been very low.

It may, then, be possible to make the tentative generalization that in a highly developed industrial society under conditions of decreasing unemployment there will be some movement toward more regular employment patterns and greater conformity to conventionally defined "full-time" work weeks by a larger fraction of the work force, along with less intermittency of employment.

How much part-time and intermittent work was there in the United States at the turn of the century? The first thing that must be said is that there is no body of nationwide evi-

[8] Special Labor Force Report No. 48, *Work Experience of the Population in 1963* (Washington, D.C.: U.S. Department of Labor, Bureau of Labor Statistics), p. 10.

dence on work experience that can be confidently relied upon to throw light on this question. The great mass of heterogeneous data which appears to say something about hours around the turn of the century—and which has therefore helped to give the impression of long hours worked by so many people —is largely beside the point since it is so uniformly composed of data of scheduled full-time weeks. Of course such data do tell us a good deal about American industrial practice of the time. Factories and workshops, mines and mills indubitably did open early in the morning and closed their gates at early evening hours rather than late in the afternoon. Scheduled full-time hours at the turn of the century show remarkable uniformity, centering around the figure of sixty hours, with exceptions being much more apt to be above the figure than below.

But again it must be emphasized that these data do not help to answer our question. In the first place, they are not about actual hours worked. In the second place, they tend to be overwhelmingly confined to "manufacturing industries." They tell us nothing about continuity of employment over the year, nothing about whether the work force worked every day of the week, nothing about absenteeism, about turnover, about tenure. They merely confirm the tendency, already so strong when we cast our eye in cursory fashion over early industrial history, to see the "industrial revolution" of a country in terms of a heroic, if also tragic, myth: "dark satanic mills" teeming with men, women, and children who toiled unremittingly at their machines.

THE CASE OF ENGLAND

It comes as something of a shock to be reminded that in the country in which this myth emerged, England of the early nineteenth century, approximately only one worker in eighty was employed in that most typical of factories, the cotton textile mill. Indeed a prominent theme of English economic historians of this period is the immense problem faced by entrepreneurs in creating a disciplined industrial labor force. Part of the horror which today is felt when the practices of the employer are examined is that this element of *discipline,* so ruthlessly imposed, seemed necessary to contemporaries if an industrial labor force was to be had at all.

But admittedly we know all too little of the industrial labor force of England in these early years of industrialization, little about its exact proportions in comparison to the entire body of working men and women, industrial and agricultural, rural and urban, casual and regular. However, at a later period in England's history, just before the end of the nineteenth century, when it was agreed that England was the very model of the industrialized society, we can get some impression—admittedly only an impression—of the work experience at least of the urban labor force from the various surveys of urban life, particularly the great study of London, Charles Booth's *Life and Labour of the People in London.*[9]

The London of the late 1880s that is the subject of Booth's investigation was of course not typical of England. It was less industrial than cities such as Birmingham and Manchester, although it had its great industries. It was more commercial than the rest of England, although the importance of commercial activities in other large English cities should not therefore be underestimated. But above all London was more completely urbanized and had been so for a much longer period.

What does *Life and Labour of the People in London* say about the character of work experience from the point of view of our investigation?

[9] Charles Booth, *Life and Labour of the People in London* (2d ed.; London and New York: Macmillan and Co., Ltd., 1892–97), 9 vols.

What stands out is the extent to which Booth, who was primarily interested in the question of poverty, came to view the great part of London poverty, the overwhelming and appalling mass of the poor, as directly related to what our investigation calls the peripherality of the labor force. It is true that Booth may have overemphasized the directness of this relationship. He confesses, for example, that his object "has been to attempt to show the numerical relation which poverty, misery, and depravity bear to *regular* earnings." [10]

First of all let us examine what he has to say about the district which is called East London. Here is Booth's description of the area, and along with it an admission of a basic problem which arises when an investigation of "peripherality" of any kind is being made, a problem which arises, for example, in something as basic as contemporary U.S. census efforts to obtain an accurate enumeration of young male Negroes in urban centers:

The special difficulty of making an accurate picture of so shifting a scene as the low-class streets in East London present is very evident. . . . As in photographing a crowd, the details of the picture continually change, but the general effect is much the same, whatever moment is chosen. I have attempted to produce an instantaneous picture, fixing the facts of my negative as they appear at a given moment, and the imagination of my readers must add the movements, the constant changes, the whirl and turmoil of like. In many districts the people are always on the move; they shift from one part of it to another like "fish in a river." . . . On the whole, however, the people usually do not go far, and often cling from generation to generation to one vicinity, almost as if the set of streets which lie there were an isolated country village.[11]

Booth divides the population into eight categories, and it is of some interest to note that the members of three of these

10 Charles Booth, *Life and Labour of the People in London* (1st ed.; London and Edinburgh: Williams and Norgate, 1889), I, 7. Italics added.
11 *Ibid.*, pp. 26–27.

eight classes would be included in our definition of the peripheral worker. In his words the groups are:

A. The lowest class of occasional labourers, loafers and semi-criminals.
B. Casual earnings—"very poor."
C. Intermittent earnings ⎫
D. Small regular earnings ⎬ together the "poor."
E. Regular standard earnings—above the line of poverty.

The other classes tend to be given status labels:

F. Higher class labour.
G. Lower middle class.
H. Upper middle class.[12]

Booth gives fairly precise estimates of the proportion of the population made up of the various classes. He estimates that the class of "occasional labourers, loafers and semi-criminals" is about 1¼ percent of the population, but confesses that "this is no more than a very rough estimate, as these people are beyond enumeration." Their lot is not enviable. "It is not easy," remarks Booth, "to say how they live; the living is picked up, and what is got is frequently shared." He notes that their life is the "life of savages, with vicissitudes of extreme hardship and occasional excess," and, in a burst of scorn and pity, he sums them up as

the battered figures who slouch through the streets, and play the beggar or the bully, or help to foul the record of the unemployed; these are the worst class of corner men who hang round the doors of public-houses, the young men who spring forward on any chance to earn a copper, the ready material for disorder when occasion serves. They render no useful service, they create no wealth: more often they destroy it.[13]

However, Booth's second class is quite another matter. First of all, the members of it constitute a substantial part of the

[12] *Ibid.*, p. 33.   [13] *Ibid.*, p. 38.

population, slightly more than one tenth of the total. In the East London which is the subject of his concern, this tenth is dependent upon what Booth calls "casual earnings"; as a result they are very poor." They are concentrated on the docks and in transport activities in general. His description of their activities and of their labor market presents a familiar picture; it might have been written about the waterfront of New York or San Francisco before the recent efforts at decasualization. Its most prominent feature is "a large number of men, in the aggregate, who look out for work from day to day at wharves and canals, or seek employment as porters in connection with the markets."

However, Booth adds that "there seems to be more regularity about the work . . . for those who, being always on the spot, are personally known to the employers and their foremen." He notes also that the condition of this group of casual laborers is "a test of the condition of trade generally. . . . a sort of 'distress meter.' " More interestingly, Booth sees the problem as related both to the demand for and the supply of labor of this particular kind. On the one hand the workers "do not, on the average, get as much as three days' work a week," but he adds, "it is doubtful if many of them could or would work full time for long together if they had the opportunity." They are a kind of anomaly in an industrial society, an indigestible lump.

The ideal of such persons is to work when they like and play when they like; these it is who are rightly called the "leisure class" among the poor—leisure bounded very closely by the pressure of want, but habitual to the extent of second nature. They cannot stand the regularity and dullness of civilized existence, and find the excitement they need in the life of the streets, or at home as spectators of or participants in some highly coloured domestic scene.[14]

[14] *Ibid.*, pp. 42–43.

Recall, however, that the same group is composed partly of those who have been in London clinging "from generation to generation to one vicinity, almost as if the set of streets which lie there were an isolated country village." [15] It seems clear that the creation of a disciplined industrial working class is not always the inevitable result of urbanization. Some at least of the urban population can become sidetracked into areas and activities that have little of the discipline and order which characterize the factory and live instead, contrary to the myth of the industrial revolution, as if in an "isolated country village."

The casual worker of Class B is more or less a part-time worker. His work becomes more part time as the economy approaches "bad times." The excess supply of this type of worker has the desirable economic function of enabling a critical element of the economy, the transfer and distribution of goods, to accommodate itself to the necessarily intermittent character of modern transportation technology, epitomized by the arrival and departure of the large steamship. Indeed, it seems probable that from a purely technological point of view the necessity of having a large pool of labor in excess of day-by-day needs in order to service transportation vehicles was less marked in the period before the modern barge, freight train, and steamship. Of course the London coasting trade, particularly the coal trade, must have made it necessary to have a considerable stand-by supply of labor long before the "industrial revolution" of the late eighteenth century. Even such a vehicle as the stagecoach required a stand-by group of hostlers and porters.

But it should be noted that Booth believed that the cost of maintaining this pool of casual labor was more or less willingly borne by the laborers themselves as the "price" that had to be

[15] *Ibid.*, p. 27.

paid to avoid "the regularity and dullness of civilized existence."

The third category, another type of peripheral worker, is the group characterized by "intermittent earnings." According to Booth, about 8 percent of the population is in this category. Class C, combined with the two lower classes, accounts for some 20 percent of the population. The members of Class C are a very different group, however. They are, says Booth, "more than any others the victims of competition, and on them falls with particular severity the weight of recurrent depressions of trade." [16] In other words, this group performs the economic function, above all, of providing for variations of labor input to accommodate the business cycle and random ups and downs of trade. The members of Class C are prone to excessive weekly hours when they do find work; they form the central core of the "sweated" laborers.

So much for Booth's snapshot of a portion of the London labor force and his attempt to give some quantitative dimensions to it. According to these estimates, about one worker in five in East London during the late 1880s was part of a class, all of whose members were perforce peripheral, either part-time or intermittent workers, but whose social characteristics ranged all the way from the "semi-criminal" to the desperately hard-working mother, trying to create an isle of respectability for a family in the midst of crushing poverty and subject to the devastation of highly intermittent work.

They were also *all* urban, many of them for generations. Some of them were members of that category that Alfred Marshall labeled the residuum, whom he considered to be so powerless, so feckless, and so self-perpetuating that he was willing to entertain the most drastic limitations of personal freedom to remove them from urban centers.

Marshall's description of this fraction of the London labor-

[16] *Ibid.*, p. 44.

ing population, more colored by strong Victorian moral pre-conceptions than that of Charles Booth, adds further detail to this picture of the labor force of London in the late 1800s. In an article published in *The Contemporary Review* in 1884 entitled "Where to House the London Poor," [17] Marshall points out that London has an enormous attractive force that pulls to it "from far and wide many different classes of people." Among people drawn to London "by a legitimate ambition" are "many of the finest workers in the country," but unfortunately other reasons bring to London "many at the opposite end of the industrial scale." [18]

Crowds of people go there because they are impatient and reckless, or miserable and purposeless; and because they hope to prey on the charities, the follies, and the vices that are nowhere so richly gilded as there.[19]

London is a demoralizing influence and physically it debilitates its working population. "Residence for many generations amid smoke, and with scarcely any of the pure gladness of bright sunshine and green fields, gradually lowers the physical constitution." [20] Any decrease in the income of a family leads to the deterioration of the family. Moral and physical corruption go hand in hand.

Doubtless many of the poor things that crouch for hire at the doors of London workshops are descended from vigorous ancestors, and owe their degradation partly to misfortune and partly to the taste for drink that misfortune at once begets under the joyless London sky. . . . The descendants of the dissolute are naturally weak, and especially those of the dissolute in large towns. It is appalling to think of how many of the poor of London are descendants of the dissolute.[21]

As a result, London has a labor force containing "large numbers of people with poor physique, and a feeble will, with

[17] Reprinted in A. C. Pigou, ed., *Memorials of Alfred Marshall* (London: Macmillan and Co., Ltd., 1925), pp. 142–51
[18] *Ibid.*, p. 144.   [19] *Ibid.*   [20] *Ibid.*   [21] *Ibid.*

no enterprise, no courage, no hope, and scarcely any self-respect, whom misery drives to work for lower wages than the same work gets in the country." But these low wages do not benefit the employer. Instead they simply permit him to pay high rents. And a "fundamental evil" develops. The evil is that industries that should not be located in London because of any real locational advantage that London possesses nevertheless do remain in London because a depressed and debilitated segment of London's labor force will accept such low wage rates and such highly intermittent earnings. It is, says Marshall,

unreasonable, and a sign of social disease, that these [industries] should be housed in London. The industries that thus linger on are chiefly those in which the workers are scattered, not able easily to organize themselves, and most at the mercy of the unscrupulous employer; those industries, in short, which are shunned by the hearty and strong, and are the refuge of the weak and broken-spirited.[22]

Marshall goes on to discuss London's industries, the distribution of which "is indeed just what would naturally follow from the causes that . . . determine the character of its population." He groups industries in two categories, the first of which performs work that must be done in London. In 1884 there were, according to Marshall, some 400,000 domestic servants, including 50,000 washerwomen. About 150,000 laborers are engaged in "carrying and storage."[23] More than a hundred thousand are employed in the construction industry. And almost one hundred thousand of London's labor force are what he calls "general laborers." All these workers perform work that must perforce be done in London. Marshall feels that in these instances "the supply of labour conforms itself to the demand, and is not affected by the special character of the population of London."[24]

But for other industries located in London where the city

[22] *Ibid.*, p. 145.   [23] *Ibid.*   [24] *Ibid.*

has no peculiar locational advantages and there is no impelling reason why the work has to be carried on in the city, "the supply of labour is determined by the character of the population, and the demand follows the supply." [25] Some of these industries pay high wages and constitute no problem. But there are "a great many minor industries, mostly very small; . . . the greater part are very poorly paid." Marshall points out that "the total number of those engaged in them, though much less than is often thought, is yet very considerable." [26] In addition there is one great group of industries which need not be located in London. These are the apparel trades. Most of the 150,000 employed in these industries are "very poorly paid, and do work which it is against all economic reason to have done where ground-rent is high." And as is so often the case in poorly paid industries, they have a high proportion of female workers. [27]

Marshall emphasizes that the population of the city is "already migratory in a great measure."

One out of five of those now living who were born in London has already gone elsewhere. Of those who are now in London more than a third were born elsewhere. . . . There are about 800,000 females living in London who were born elsewhere. Of these immigrants a great part do no good to themselves or to others by coming to London.[28]

It is because the immigrants "do no good to themselves or to others" that Marshall feels that very strong pressure ought to be exerted to keep potential immigrants away from London. A rigorous enforcement of housing regulations would in fact be enough to keep out a "good many shiftless people" or to induce them to go to America, "where the shiftless often become shiftful." [29]

Moreover, since many of the industries which employ the

25 *Ibid.*, p. 146.   26 *Ibid.*   27 *Ibid.*   28 *Ibid.*, p. 147.
29 *Ibid.*

most poorly paid of London's laboring population are uneco-
nomic, since the supply of their workers is created not by the
demand for such workers but by the underlying physical and
moral character of a significant portion of London's population, it is economically justifiable to intervene quite forcefully
to alter the supply and demand conditions in these industries.
Marshall does not hold out any real hope that their condition
can improve in London itself. "The very weak and poorly
paid," he declares, "want help." [30] They are indeed in a worse
case than a horse would be:

If they were horses, they would get [help] fast enough; a weak
horse is sent off into the country, where stableroom is cheap.
. . . Surely time and money devoted to helping the feeble and
timid to move and carry their work with them are better spent
than in diminishing some of the evils of their lives in London. In
London, even when their houses are whitewashed, the sky will be
dark . . . they will go on deteriorating; and, as to their children,
the more of them will grow up to manhood the lower will be the
average physique and the average morality of the coming English
generation.[31]

Marshall's solution, therefore, includes the establishment of
committees to assist the London poor to emigrate from London to the country. The committees are

to interest themselves in the formation of a colony in some place
well beyond the range of London smoke. After seeing their way
to building or buying suitable cottages there, they would enter into
communication with some of the employers of low-waged labour.
They would select at first industries that use very little fixed
capital. . . . Fortunately it happens that most of the industries
which it is important to move are of this kind.[32]

The net result of Marshall's scheme would be a decrease in the
supply of labor in London and a consequent tendency for
wages to rise to some extent in London itself. The emigrants
would still be low wage earners, but their standard of living

---

[30] *Ibid.*, p. 146.   [31] *Ibid.*, pp. 146–47.   [32] *Ibid.*, p. 149.

would increase in two ways: first, because the proportion of their income going to house rent would decrease; second, because their surroundings would be more healthy and pleasurable.

Nothing came directly of Marshall's proposal about "where to house the London poor." But it reveals quite vividly the extent of Marshall's concern about a portion of London's population in the 1880s, many of whom were peripheral workers in our sense of the term, either because of the highly intermittent character of their earnings or because of the fact that they were part-time workers. So serious did Marshall regard the problem that he was willing to entertain the idea of quite rigorous intervention in the lives of the London poor and was willing also to claim that in their case the operation of the labor market was in a profound sense perverse. The supply of labor did not respond to the market demand. Instead it was determined by an urban environment that so debilitated and demoralized a portion of the population that there would be an oversupply of workers at real wages which fell below what decency could be allowed to permit and which were, in fact, below what the real wages of these same workers would be if they were moved to a more favorable environment.

THE PERIPHERAL WORKER IN AMERICA
AT THE TURN OF THE CENTURY

Much the same picture, perhaps even more highly colored, could be drawn for any of the large American urban centers of the turn of the century. Several features of the cities themselves should be noticed. First of all, they were expanding with enormous rapidity. New York, for example, gained almost 50 percent in population between 1880 and 1890, increasing from 1 million to a million and a half. The urban population for the United States as a whole increased from 14 million in 1880 to

42 million in 1910.[33] This increased population was largely the result of two streams flowing into the cities, the European immigrant and the American farm boy (and girl in good measure). Both streams tended to be young, unmarried, and unindustrial in background.

Second, the very pronounced internal migration of the time should be noted. In part it was simply one manifestation of the westward movement that was to populate a continent, but there was undoubtedly a high degree of migration between urban centers, a remarkable fluidity of the population. The westward movement was met by a counterflow eastward. Dreiser's early novels celebrate this eastward flow and emphasize its rural-urban character. But it was interurban as well.

The life histories of workers to be found in Ginzberg and Berman's *The American Worker in the Twentieth Century* bring out the ceaseless change of circumstance, employment, domicile, and occupation of workers whose lives spanned the turn of the century. One worker's story provides a vivid glimpse of the character of hiring practices of the time, particularly their casualness and randomness (randomness modified by ethnic influences). A Lithuanian is speaking (he has landed in Chicago soon after his arrival in the United States):

One morning my friends woke me up at five o'clock and said, "Now, if you want life, liberty and happiness . . . you must . . . get a job. . . ." And we went to the yards. Men and women were walking in by thousands. . . . We went to the doors of one big slaughter house. There was a crowd of about 200 men waiting there for a job. They looked hungry and kept watching the door. At last a special policeman came out and began pointing to men. . . . Twenty-three were taken. Then they all went inside and all the others turned their faces away and looked tired. I remember one boy sat down and cried, just next to me, on a pile of boards.

[33] U.S. Bureau of the Census, *Historical Statistics of the United States, Colonial Times to 1957* (Washington, D.C.: Government Printing Office, 1960), p. 14.

. . . Some Lithuanians . . . told me they had come every morning for three weeks.[34]

He then bribes a "special policeman" to give him a job:

I held this job six weeks and then I was turned off. I think some other man had paid for my job, or perhaps I was too slow. . . . Now, when I was idle, I began to look about, and everywhere I saw sharp men beating out slow men like me. . . . At home we never made a man sign contract papers. We only had him make the sign of a cross and promise he would do what he said. But this was no good in Chicago. . . . I felt very bad and sorrowful in that month. I kept walking around with many other Lithuanians who had no job. Our money was going and we could find nothing to do. At night we got homesick for our fine green mountains.[35]

He then becomes a political hanger-on and is rehired by the stockyards but now has some degree of protection:

Even when work was slack I was all right, because they got me a job in the street cleaning department. . . . All of us were telling our friends to come soon. Soon they came—even thousands. The employers in the yard liked this, because those sharp foremen are inventing new machines and the work is easier to learn, and so these slow Lithuanians and even green girls can learn to do it, and then the Americans and Germans and Irish are put out.[36]

Finally he becomes a member of the Cattle Butcher's Union and his employment then apparently becomes more regular; as he puts it, "the work is evened up . . . I do not have to pay to get a job and I cannot be discharged unless I am no good." [37]

Such case histories provide an invaluable sense of the quality of life, the variety of experience, and the complexity of attitudes of workers whose lives span the period we are interested in. In many instances it is clear from the context that the experience of a worker is an experience shared in some in-

[34] Eli Ginzberg and Hyman Berman, *The American Worker in the Twentieth Century: A History Through Autobiographies* (Glencoe, Ill.: The Free Press, 1963), pp. 47–48.
[35] *Ibid.*, pp. 48–49.   [36] *Ibid.*, p. 49.   [37] *Ibid.*, p. 51.

stances by thousands, that the person recounting his work life feels that what he experienced was more or less typical of his "kind."

The vast body of material issued by various state labor departments and by bureaus or commissions of labor in the last decades of the nineteenth century and the early years of the twentieth has been for the most part left to gather dust. A thorough sifting of this material would reveal much about the actual hours worked by various occupational, industrial, and demographic groups in some of the states. Formidable difficulties, however, stand in the way of using these bits and scraps of evidence to create a mosaic which might give us a comprehensive nationwide picture. The material was collected at different times, with different purposes, with different survey techniques, and there is of course now no possibility of checking the actual questionnaires used in these surveys or the sampling techniques.

In the absence of material collected in a systematic and comprehensive fashion, it will not be possible, as noted previously, to say anything precise about the actual proportions of part-time or intermittent work experience at the turn of the century, either as a fraction of the total work experience of the population or of work experience by occupation or industry or demographic group. Like so many questions which we should now like to answer about the past, this question has only emerged out of the needs of the recent past. The absence of work experience data for the pre-World War II period is as distressing to the historian as the absence of reliable unemployment figures.

COMMITMENT TO WORK

There is another aspect of "peripherality" of work experience which, although it has undoubtedly manifested itself historically in the form of irregular employment experience and part-time work, is by its very nature not readily susceptible of quantification. Commitment to the world of work can clearly be to an occupation, an industry, or a firm. It can be the product of internal pressures—a "discipline of work" or "vocation," much in the sense that Max Weber considered that the economic importance of Protestantism lay in large part in the fact that it tied the individual firmly to a world of work because of an internalization of religious sanctions. Commitment, on the other hand, can be the result of external pressures or institutional arrangements, an example being the tying of a worker to a firm through such means as unvested pensions or seniority.

In one way or another most people have probably been strongly committed to work in Western society, the only prominent exceptions perhaps being such special classes as the landed aristocracy or such special demographic groups as the gypsies. However, it is important to emphasize that commitment to a particular kind of work, agricultural activity for example, is not necessarily something that is easily shifted to another quite different type of work. The set of rules and customs related to kinship, religion, and community that tie an individual into the productive activity of an ongoing agricultural community may be largely inoperative in the environment of an industrial society.

A necessary step in an individual's transition from an agricultural society to an industrial society may therefore take the form of a kind of decommitment-recommitment period. The decommitment will probably largely take place within the old agricultural society, produced by some breakdown in that society which hits some group with unusual severity. This process has been analyzed by James Slotkin, a cultural anthropologist at the University of Chicago, in his monograph *From*

Field to Factory, published shortly before his untimely death in 1958.[38]

Slotkin had earlier been interested in the phenomenon of the Peyote religion among American Indians of the Midwest, an interest which led him to study the process of their acculturation to industrial society. He was drawn into an investigation of what was then happening to native whites from the agricultural Southeast who were being employed in considerable numbers in certain Chicago factories. His monograph is an effort to develop a systematic body of generalizations, derived from an anthropological approach to the process of acculturation, which would be as useful in handling the experience of southern white workers exposed to Chicago industrial life as for Bantu tribesmen drawn into African mining communities. If his analysis of the process of acculturation involved in fashioning an industrial worker out of individuals who come out of a nonindustrial background is more or less correct, some of his generalizations can be used to throw additional light on the experiences of a large segment of the American working class at the turn of the century.

Let us consider again what was happening in those years in broad outline. A very large number of immigrants were arriving each year, a large proportion of whom were drawn from incompletely industrialized societies and from marginal groups within those selfsame societies, groups which were being induced to leave their age-old communities and ancient traditions simply because the old society had become disorganized and "inadequate" in some fundamental respect as far as they were concerned. In other words, a considerable fraction of these immigrants had been exposed to a prior shock of great severity which had been sufficient to dislodge them from their communities and from the supporting customs and institutions

---

[38] James Slotkin, *From Field to Factory: New Industrial Employees* (Glencoe, Ill.: The Free Press, 1960).

associated with those communities. Oscar Handlin's *The Up-rooted* provides a vivid and sympathetic account of the successive ordeals through which the immigrant passed.

The cumulative effect of massive immigration upon American life was bound to be profound and widely ramified. Extremely variable year by year, the totals for most years in the 1880s were well over 500,000. [39] This rate was maintained for the first two years of the 1890s, slackening off somewhat for the rest of the decade. At the turn of the century began the very rapid increase in immigration that was to carry the annual figures to the one million mark and over for a number of the years between 1900 and 1914. Between 1880 and 1914, 20.3 million immigrants arrived in America, an average of more than 600,000 per year. When we recall that the civilian labor force numbered probably only slightly more than 27 million in 1900 and that close to 40 percent of this total was made up of agriculturalists, some idea of the extent to which the urban industrial labor force was created in large part out of this flow of immigration can be sensed.

Data about the occupational background of the immigrants are relevant to our theme. In the early years of the period under examination, the 1880s, a good deal more than half of the immigrants were listed at the time of their arrival as having "no occupation" and a fourth were listed as laborers. The skilled worker accounted for only about one tenth of the total up to 1900. Those listed as farmers accounted for approximately another tenth. As the occupation data become more precise beginning in 1899, we find that, with the exception of a category labeled "craftsmen, foremen, operatives, and kindred workers," the great bulk of the immigrants are either unskilled or listed as having "no occupation." It seems probable, more-

[39] The historical statistics on this and succeeding pages are drawn from U.S. Bureau of the Census, *Historical Statistics of the United States.*

over, that some of the "craftsmen *et al.*" category represented relatively unskilled "new industrial" workers from Europe who were to finish their acculturation to the industrial process in the New World because it seemed to offer more promise.

While immigrants flowed into the urban industrial society of America at the turn of the century, another stream of population, this composed of native white farm boys and farm girls, also was flowing into the cities. There is no question but that the native American rural stream possessed very real advantages in the struggle for status in the rapidly expanding cities. The stream of immigrants, moreover, was becoming increasingly composed of immigrant groups whose religious and social customs had been formed in societies quite different from the dominant white Protestant northwestern European culture of the United States.

The cities themselves possessed a most inadequate administrative structure to cope with the problems of the new immigrant and usually provided almost no support to him. The immigrant was therefore dependent upon the assistance that could be provided by those of his own ethnic group who had managed to find a foothold previously. But even among his ethnic group there were those who were all too ready to batten upon his inexperience and defenselessness. Immigrant labor was rounded up in the cities for all sorts of construction and mining work, and for many new immigrants this meant unsettling trips to labor camps and the life of the labor gang with its inherent instability and rootlessness.

In other words, the process of commitment, the movement from uncommitment to commitment, was made more brutal and therefore more destabilizing for a portion of the immigrant population because it was accompanied in America by the growth of large, socially disorganized urban complexes on the one hand and the vast movement across the continent of a good part of the population, particularly of the immigrant stream, on the other. What is more, the initial tasks that awaited many of these immigrants were in just those sectors of the economy that have historically been most irregular in their employment patterns.

There was the enormous task of providing housing for the vast expansion of population in old eastern cities and for the millions swarming into the new cities being thrust up in the Midwest and West. There was the immense task involved in the completion of the railroad network. In 1880 all the track in the country was estimated to run to 115,647 miles. By 1900 the figure had risen to 258,784 miles and a good portion of the original 115,647 had been relaid, since it was American practice to place relatively light rails initially, and the subsequent tremendous increase in rail traffic now justified a more or less complete reconstruction of the original network.

The railroad construction gangs were one means by which many of the "new industrial" workers were absorbed (and in the process a good many destroyed). But they were not an ideal mechanism for shaping the full-time, full-year worker. Moreover, the vast expansion of the internal market that had taken place in the last decades of the nineteenth century had necessitated a parallel increase in the interstices of the railroad network, and this of course was provided by an expansion of local transportation facilities, almost all of which were horse-drawn. The extent to which the commercial areas of cities swarmed with draymen and porters at the turn of the century can best be realized from the figures of horse-drawn vehicles produced in a typical year at the turn of the century. In 1899, 570,000 farm wagons, trucks, and business vehicles were produced and 905,000 carriages, buggies, and sulkies. The number of teamsters alone, who account for only a fraction of those whose activities centered around this transportation-distribution system, was given as 374,000 in 1900. Another 84,000 laborers are listed as engaged in transportation other than railroads. What they did is not clear. However, it seems probable that a good deal of this transportation activity was necessarily intermittent, part time, plagued by casual employment.

Such occupations, along with the 117,000 lumbermen, raftsmen, and wood choppers, provided a demand for workers who were in the process of developing commitment to the work force. Incidentally there was a very large number of men who worked in sawmills, but the 1900 census data unfortunately lump them with another category, those who produced "miscellaneous wood products," so that it is not possible to say exactly how many they numbered.[40]

Construction has historically been one of the bridges between an agricultural society and culture and the industrial society. The Irish navvy of the nineteenth century is merely one example of such a hybrid worker. Indeed, it is because construction takes place in a largely unconfined surrounding, for the most part out of doors, and is characterized by considerable variety of scene and intermittency of effort that it appeals to the agriculturalist who is moving into industrial society and at the same time demands his particular virtues and strengths.

The extraordinary amount of construction activity at the

[40] The occupational data for 1900 are often very frustrating from our point of view. For example, the series entitled "Laborers (not elsewhere classified)—construction" provides us with the following information. In 1900, 20,000 workers were so employed, but the figure jumps to 531,000 in 1910, to 1,340,000 in 1940, slackening off to 788,000 in 1950. Clearly something is very much awry with the figures but unfortunately they are given this way both in David Kaplan and M. Claire Casey, *Occupational Trends in the United States, 1900 to 1950* (Washington, D.C.: U.S. Department of Commerce, 1958), and in U.S. Bureau of the Census, *Historical Statistics of the United States*. This discrepancy is particularly disheartening since the construction laborer has been one of the occupational groups most subject to intermittent employment and it is likely that this occupational category was more intermittent in 1900 than it is today. The industry as a whole was probably more apt to be in the grips of climate than it is today. At least some of the technological changes which have taken place since 1900 have been designed to permit more steady productive activity in the industry.

turn of the century demanded a great deal more simple unskilled labor, hired by the day to accomplish tasks that were
soon finished, than it does today. The hod carrier and the
ditchdigger, even the relatively skilled bricklayer, come to
mind.

If there is merit in the view that the relatively uncommitted
worker, the "new industrial" worker of Slotkin, is prone to
irregular employment patterns,[41] regardless of where he may
come from, then it would seem that it is even more likely that
the turn of the century in comparison with our own day was
characterized by a vast body of workers who properly would
belong in "the peripheral labor force" from the point of view
of their degree of commitment to occupation, industry, and
firm. We might add one further consideration. Our analysis
says that any group which comes out of a different society and
enters the industrial world suffers initially a period of relative
disorganization with accompanying intermittency of employment patterns.

Youth necessarily passes through such a period, even if only
in a moderate degree. Youth must give up its commitment to
childhood (with all the customs and supporting agencies that
are associated with such status) and enter a new world. Now
to the extent that working lives were short, to the extent that
immigration contained differentially more late adolescents than
the population as a whole, to the extent that it was the farm
boy and *girl* who made the jump to the city, we would expect
the age distribution of the working force to emphasize the
"peripheral" character of the labor force of the late nineteenth
century and the early decades of the twentieth.

The concept of the process of commitment, either as Kerr
has developed it with specific reference to the process of economic development,[42] or in its more general form as it is

[41] Slotkin, *From Field to Factory*, pp. 33–43.
[42] Clark Kerr, *Labor and Management in Industrial Society* (Garden
City, N.Y.: Doubleday and Company, 1964), Part IV.

presented in Slotkin's work, sees the problem in terms which are outside the usual considerations of the economist. An individual's presence in the "peripheral labor force," from Slotkin's point of view, does not really represent an economic choice at all. Rather it is a relatively inevitable part of the life cycle of an individual who is attempting to move within his own lifetime between two very different cultural situations. He is prone to intermittent, part-time activity because that is for the while his cultural "nature." If he is to be eventually absorbed into the industrial labor force, the industrial society must either want his kind of work activity or at the very least make room for him in the sense of accommodating itself to his predispositions.

-≺ CHAPTER III ≻-

A STATISTICAL OVERVIEW: MAJOR AGGREGATES AND TRENDS

THE CIVILIAN LABOR FORCE in 1965 numbered on the average slightly more than 75.5 million people of whom on the average slightly more than 72 million were employed. The fact that the number of people in the labor force is usually given as an annual average masks the large variation that takes place on a more or less regular seasonal basis in the monthly figures. The labor force is a body whose composition is constantly changing but at the nucleus of which is a large and stable mass, the full-time, full-year workers. Subtracting the 48.3 million full-time, full-year workers in 1965 from the rest of the labor force gives us a group whose composition and size changes, ranging somewhere between 25 and 30 million.

Moreover, it is possible to subtract from this group of 25 to 30 million individuals another stable element, those workers who are part-time workers all year round. This second group of full-year workers numbered about 5.4 million in 1965. Totaling all workers who worked full-year schedules, whether full time or part time, we find that, of the 86.2 million who had work experience of some kind in 1965, about 53.7 million were continuously in the labor force and employed. All those whose labor force status shifted from employment to unemployment at some time during 1965 or who entered or left the labor force one or more times during the year were contained in a group of some 32.5 million, of whom some 3.5 million on the average were unemployed.

Of individuals with part-time work experience, about 9 million in 1965 worked no more than half the year, and of this group almost two thirds, or some 5.5 million, had work experience for no more than a quarter of the year. In other words, a good deal more than half of those individuals whose work experience in 1965 was limited to 13 weeks or less were also part-time workers. Among the rest of the workers who collectively made up the peripheral labor force in 1965 were the proportionately very large group of full-time workers who had more than half a year of work experience, some 12 million workers, about 7 million of whom had at least 40 weeks of work experience during the year. A final group, the part-time workers who worked more than half the year but less than the full year, numbered slightly more than 3 million. A pattern therefore is clear when we look at the "peripheral labor force" as a whole. That portion of it which is composed of full-time workers tends to be rather evenly distributed by number of weeks worked. In marked contrast, the part-time worker also tends to have fewer weeks of work experience.

The subgroups we have distinguished represent very different degrees of "peripherality," involve very different segments of the population, and raise very different problems from the point of view of public policy. The following is a rather arbitrary classification of these subgroups in 1965 by "degree of peripherality":

	Number (in millions)	Percent of Total Peripheral Labor Force
Slightly Peripheral		
40–49 weeks, full time	6.6	17
Moderately Peripheral		
27–39 weeks, full time	4.7	
Full year, part time	5.4	
40–49 weeks, part time	1.5	
Subtotal	11.6	31
Severely Peripheral		
26 weeks or less, full time	9.1	
27–39 weeks, part time	1.8	
26 weeks or less, part time	8.8	
Subtotal	13.6	52

The "severely peripheral" group might usefully be broken down further into these two categories:

Moderately Severely Peripheral		
14–26 weeks, full time	4.3	
27–39 weeks, part time	1.8	
Subtotal	6.1	16
Extremely Peripheral		
26 weeks or less, part-time	8.8	
13 weeks or less, full time	4.8	
Subtotal	13.6	36

The roughness of the above system of classification does not need to be emphasized, but it may serve to focus attention upon the great variation in degree of peripherality while at the same time giving some impression of the extent to which very peripheral attachment to the world of work is indeed a major component of the peripheral labor force. From a third to a half of the 38 million individuals who constituted the peripheral labor force in 1965 found work experience very much less part of their lives than did the great majority of the labor force. Those individuals in the "extremely peripheral" category constituted about one sixth of all individuals with work experience in 1965.

Peripherality, a multidimensioned phenomenon, can scarcely be pinned down with the crude two-dimensional measures which we currently possess, hours on the one hand and weeks worked on the other. To add to the complexity of the problem, conceptually we should, in theory at least, try to contend with the fact that full-time and full-year work experience have different meanings for different occupations and industries. The teacher is simply one obvious example. Is the public school teacher who does not work during the summer a full-year worker? What constitutes full-time hours for this profession? What about the surgeon, the baseball player, the musician?

Nevertheless, if we concentrate for the time being only on the more objective qualities of peripheral work experience, particularly the extent of a worker's involvement purely in a time sense in an occupation or industry, postponing any consideration of such subjective elements of peripherality as, for example, its "voluntary" or "involuntary" character, these two measures, hours of work experience per week and weeks worked per year, clearly do yield rather striking divisions of the total population.

It should, moreover, be borne in mind that peripherality, like so many other qualities of the population, tends to be least definable when it becomes most extreme, i.e., when an individual has no work experience. Such individuals, who may or may not be in the labor force, are really not definable by occupation or industry in any clear-cut and unambiguous sense. Our view of the labor force is much like that of the field of vision of the nearsighted. Those areas of vision which are central are relatively clear. These include particularly the full-time, full-year worker. The more extremely any group differs from this full-time, full-year group, the more its exact features become somewhat blurred, particularly along the occupational and industrial axes.

In addition to those individuals who have had some work experience, though not full time and full year, and are therefore included in the "peripheral labor force" by our working definition, there is another group of workers who were in the labor force at some time during the year but did not work at all. Such individuals, numbering close to 1.5 million in 1965, should logically be considered to be peripheral workers. About a third of this group were teen-agers. Another group which should undoubtedly be included in the "peripheral labor force" is composed of workers who have withdrawn from the labor force but would reenter it if opportunities for employment were to improve. This group includes those who have withdrawn from the labor force because they were unwilling to accept substandard wages and working conditions or because they were unwilling to take what they considered to be "dead end" jobs.

Finally, an unknown, but possibly appreciable amount of the most extremely peripheral work experience never gets reported at all in the statistics of work experience. The investigations of Liebhafsky have demonstrated that it is not possible with the usual techniques of statistical survey to determine the labor force status and the work experience of the most disadvantaged individuals in society, particularly the nonwhite workers of the smaller urban centers of the South, where thousands of Negroes, formerly engaged in marginal agricultural activity, have collected together to form pools of labor available for the most casual and temporary types of employment but would never qualify for inclusion in the labor force according to current definitions of job-seeking activity.[1]

THE FULL-TIME WORKER AND THE REMAINDER OF THE WORK FORCE

The peripheral labor force constitutes an extremely heterogeneous group, so heterogeneous that no label comes conveniently to mind for it except the awkward one we are using, one, however, which serves to emphasize the fact that this group is united only by the fact that for one reason or another its members do not choose, or are not permitted, to devote to work the amount of time which is conventionally termed full time in the industry or occupation in which they are employed.

To draw attention to the major dimensions of peripheral work experience of the population in proportion to all work experience, a matrix is used whose rows contain weeks of work experience and whose columns are divided between full-time and part-time work experience. The February work experience survey of the Current Population Survey does not attempt to break down hours per week into finer categories than full time and part time. Moreover, the reader should bear in mind that a worker is classified part time if he "worked at jobs which provided less than 35 hours per week in a majority of the weeks in which he worked." Since the number of hours an individual has worked may have varied from week to week, a classification scheme with a more detailed breakdown of hours worked per week than is used in the *Work Experience Reports* would be seriously misleading. It would, for example, tempt the user of the data to assume that peripheral work

[1] See E. E. Liebhafsky, *A Methodological Approach to Identification and Classification of Certain Types of Inactive Work Seekers* (Houston, Texas: University of Houston, Center for Research in Business and Economics, 1965), pp. 1–34.

experience is much more stable than it is in fact. In Table 3.1 the percentage distribution of all persons who had any work experience during 1965 is presented in the simple matrix form just outlined. Several points, mentioned earlier in passing, may well bear reemphasizing.

Table 3.1. *Percentage Distribution of All Individuals with Work Experience in 1965 by Hours and Weeks*

Weeks Worked

Hours per Week	13 or Less	14–26	27–39	40–47	48–49	50–52	Total
Full time (35 and more)	5.6	5.0	5.4	4.9	2.7	56.1	79.7
Part time (less than 35)	6.4	3.8	2.1	1.2	0.5	6.3	20.3
Total	12.0	8.8	7.5	6.1	3.2	62.4	100.0

Source: Special Labor Force Report No. 76, *Work Experience of the Population in 1965* (Washington, D.C.: U.S. Department of Labor, Bureau of Labor Statistics), Table A-1, p. A-5.

First of all, the matrix brings out clearly the wide variety of work experience. Although the full-time, full-year cell stands out as by far the largest, less than six out of ten workers have had this kind of work experience in all the years that work experience data have been collected. However, almost four out of five individuals do have primarily full-time work experience, although one out of eight individuals with full-time work experience worked a half year or less in 1965.

One out of five individuals has primarily part-time work experience. Of these part-time workers, one half worked a half year or less; one third, 13 weeks or less.

If we turn our attention to those persons who, whether full-time or part-time workers, did not work a full year, we find that one out of every five persons with work experience in

1965 worked a half year or less. One out of six worked between 27 and 49 weeks, but of this group the overwhelming majority were full-time workers. Those full-time workers who do not work a full year are rather evenly distributed, as we observed earlier, among the other weeks-worked cells of the matrix. Part-time workers, however, tend to work either a full year or a half year or less.

Table 3.2. *Percentage Distribution of All Individuals with Work Experience, 1960 to 1966, by Hours and Weeks*

		Weeks Worked		
Hours per Week	*Year*	*1–26*	*27–49*	*50–52*
Full time				
(35 and more)	1960	10.9	15.0	53.7
	1961	11.4	15.0	53.6
	1962	11.1	14.7	53.7
	1963	11.0	13.9	54.6
	1964	10.9	13.7	55.0
	1965	10.6	13.0	56.1
	1966	10.9	12.3	58.0
Part time				
(less than 35)	1960	9.8	4.1	6.6
	1961	9.7	3.8	6.5
	1962	10.0	4.1	6.3
	1963	10.2	4.0	6.3
	1964	10.2	4.0	6.2
	1965	10.2	3.8	6.3
	1966	8.5	3.9	6.3

Source: Special Labor Force Reports, *Work Experience of the Population.*
Note: From 1960 to 1965, the youngest age group contained persons 14 to 17 years old. In 1966, 14- and 15-year-olds were dropped. With their inclusion in the 1966 work experience data, it is estimated that the percentage of full-time, full-year work experience would have been 56.6 rather than 58.0.

An outstanding feature of this matrix is its relative stability over the years 1960–66. A slightly abbreviated matrix is presented in Table 3.2 in which comparative percentages for each cell are given for this period. In the six years from 1960 through 1965, a period of growth and decreasing rates of unemployment, most of the categories in the table remain remarkably unchanged. Beginning in 1962 there is a small increase in the percentage of total work experience which took the form of full-time work for the full year, an increase which was almost exactly counterbalanced by a decrease in the percentage share of full-time work experience 27 to 49 weeks in duration. The sudden sharp increase in full-time, full-year work experience in 1966 is probably in large part due to the redefinition of the youngest age group in the work experience data so as to exclude persons 14 and 15 years old. Since these very young workers are almost entirely part-time workers for short periods of the year, their exclusion tends to decrease the percentage share of those with part-time work experience for less than half a year while increasing percentage shares of other categories.

RECENT TRENDS IN PART-TIME AND PART-YEAR WORK EXPERIENCE

To what extent does the over-all stability of the percentage distribution of all individuals with work experience by hours and weeks mask changes in the work experience distribution of particular groups? What has happened over a longer period?

Work experience data on an annual basis are available only from the beginning of the 1950s. Chart 3.1 presents series from 1950 to 1965 for the following categories: percentage by sex of those who (a) worked at full-time jobs 50 to 52 weeks; (b) worked at full-time jobs from 1 to 26 weeks; (c) worked part time 1 to 52 weeks.

Individuals with full-time, full-year work experience as a proportion of all individuals with work experience during the year increased from about 56 percent to about 59 percent between 1950 and 1953. During the next five years this figure fell more or less steadily until it had reached slightly less than 54 percent in 1958. It remained at that level for four years and then began a slow climb in 1962 which by 1965 brought the figure to just over 56.

The total period is much too short to form the basis for even tentative generalizations about underlying trends which might be at work to alter the proportion of those in the population whose work experience is full time for the full year. Indeed, the lack of any clear-cut trend in this series over this period of time is fairly striking. The expansion of demand associated with the Korean War period seems to have pushed up the full-time, full-year percentage, and again, during the years 1962–65, a period of slowly decreasing unemployment rates, the figure slowly increased; but even with the change in the definition of the youngest group in the work experience survey from 14-17 years of age to 16-17 years of age—which, by dropping a fairly sizable group of individuals, almost none of whom had full-time, full-year work experience, therefore tended to increase the percentage of full-time, full-year work experience of the remainder—the latest available figure, that for 1966, is slightly lower than the highest figure achieved during the 1950s, 58.0 percent as against 58.9 percent.

The proportion of those at work some time during the year, whose work experience is primarily part time, rose fairly steadily from slightly under 15 percent in 1952 and 1953 to approximately 20 percent in 1958. Since that time the figure has remained almost constant. The steady rise in the figure from 1953 through 1958 seemed then to indicate that there was a strong trend for part-time work experience to increase as a proportion of total work experience. Indeed, if the rate of increase in the proportion of part-time work experience had continued at the same rate as between 1953 and 1958, almost 30

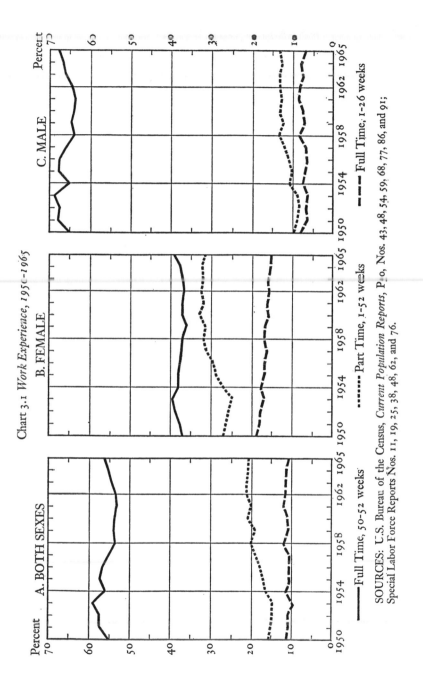

Chart 3.1 *Work Experience, 1950–1965*

A. BOTH SEXES

B. FEMALE

C. MALE

—— Full Time, 50–52 weeks

········ Part Time, 1–52 weeks

– – – Full Time, 1–26 weeks

SOURCES: U.S. Bureau of the Census, *Current Population Reports*, P-50, Nos. 43, 48, 54, 59, 68, 77, 86, and 91; Special Labor Force Reports Nos. 11, 19, 25, 38, 48, 62, and 76.

percent of individuals who work sometime during the year would now be part-time workers, rather than the present 20 percent.

The proportion of those with work experience during the year who worked full-time schedules only half the year or less remained almost constant over the entire period from 1950 to 1965, hovering around 11 percent. However, there has been a very slow increase from 1953 in the proportion of those with work experience who worked part time for a half year or less—from less than 7 percent to slightly more than 10 percent.

There are several points of difference between the record of male and female work experience during this fifteen-year period. The series which seems to show the widest year-to-year swings is that of male full-time, full-year work experience. From a high point of approximately 70 percent of all males with work experience during the year, the series fell to slightly under 64 percent in 1958, a figure which remained almost unchanged until 1962. Between 1962 and 1965 it rose to slightly more than 67 percent. Male part-time work experience rose from less than 9 percent in 1952 to 13 percent in 1958, a figure which has remained practically unchanged since then. However, male part-time work experience for a half year or less has tended to rise from 1955 to the present, from just under 4 percent to just over 6 percent.

It should be noted that, although part of the variability in the series of all male workers in contributed by workers under 24 and workers over 60, the percentage of individuals in the prime age groups whose work experience is full time for the full year is subject to quite considerable year-to-year changes. From a low point of slightly over 75 percent in 1958, the proportion of males 35 to 44 years old whose work experience has been full time for the full year has more or less steadily risen to slightly over 84 percent in 1965. For this age group it is now appreciably higher than the high point reached during the Korean War period. Another way of putting the matter is that since the proportion of all males whose work experience is full time for the full year actually decreased between 1953 and 1965 while that of prime age males increased, the younger and older male age groups have shown a tendency toward lower proportions of full-time, full-year work experience. The decrease for older males was quite rapid between 1954 and 1960. Since that time some of the older age groups have shown an actual increase in the percentage share of full-time, full-year work experience, for example, from less than 44 percent in 1960 for males 65 to 69 years old to over 49 percent in 1965.

The proportion of all females with work experience during the year who worked full time for the full year rose from about 37 percent in 1950 to slightly above 39 percent in 1953, only to be followed by six years of decline, so that in 1959 only about 36 percent of females with work experience worked full time the year round. A slight rise between 1959 and 1960 was followed by marked stability for the next three years. Beginning in 1963 a rise in the percentage has occurred which brought the proportion of women working full time for the full year to just under 39 percent in 1965. However, over this same fifteen years there has been a more or less continual, if very slow, decline in the proportion of females whose work experience has taken the form of full-time work a half year or less. In 1950 almost 19 percent of females had this kind of work experience; by 1965 only slightly more than 15 percent were so employed.

After a slight decrease between 1950 and 1953 to about 25 percent of all women with work experience, the proportion of women whose work experience was primarily part time began a sharp increase that lasted until 1958, at which time almost 32 percent of all women were in this category. Since 1958, however, there has been little change in the proportion of women who work part time. The proportion of women who work part time only a half year or less has, however, risen slightly over this period of time, so that now slightly more than 16 percent of women are part-time employees for a half year or less.

As in the case of men, the aggregate figures for women mask considerable change in the proportions of full-time, full-year workers in particular age groups over these fifteen years. A discussion of some of these changes is contained in Chapters V and VI, which deal in greater detail with the work experience of women.

⊰ CHAPTER IV ⊱

TOWARD A THEORY
OF PERIPHERALITY

THE FOREGOING CHAPTERS have sketched some of the major dimensions of peripheral work experience against a historical background. At several points elements of a general conception of the relationship between peripheral work experience and full-time, full-year work experience in the United States have emerged, but there has been no attempt to develop these in a systematic fashion. It seems appropriate at this point to bring together these elements in a tentative effort to provide a general explanation of the multifaceted phenomenon which we have characterized by the term "the peripheral worker."

THE PERIPHERAL WORKER IN AMERICA:
A HISTORICAL HYPOTHESIS

The substance of the following pages consists of a general framework within which it may be possible to find an explanation for a number of the characteristics of peripheral workers over a substantial period of time. This framework, or theory, will attempt to draw together elements from history, economics, and sociology. One of the virtues of such an approach, from the point of view of our present concerns, is that it treats the question as one involving primarily the process of forming increasingly firm commitments, on the part of both the firm and the individual, to the provision and performance of labor services. Another virtue of this approach is its emphasis on the fact that, in a highly differentiated society with an advanced economy, there are powerful societal forces tending to create a high degree of stability in a large fraction of the labor force, forces which operate both from the side of the employer and from the side of the employee. The implication of this is that in such a society a very large proportion of the work force should, in the absence of counteracting factors, follow a pattern of increasing socialization as far as commitment to work is concerned. The major institutions of society, particularly the family, will exert very powerful influences to lead the child in an orderly way to the development of attitudes toward work which assume an eventual full commitment to work. If, then, there is a considerable proportion of the population whose work experience is irregular, it is necessary to examine the interaction of the major subsystems of the total society to see how it comes about that a portion of the population is not fully integrated into the economy.

Among the important aspects of the differentiation of the working population into (a) a stable group of full-time, full-year workers and (b) a fluctuating group of part-time and intermittent workers are the characteristic attitudes that each group comes to hold about itself and about the other group. Individuals from the two groups develop pervasive expectations that tend to confirm their status. The central institutions of the labor markets will also be shaped in part by these expectations and so tend to confirm them. Eventually it will come about that the widely differing patterns of work experience displayed by individuals from these two groups seem inevitable and "natural," a rationalization serving to justify and perpetuate the patterns. What from the point of view of other societies or other times might seem inexplicable and "wrong" becomes the usual state of affairs.

In this bifurcation of the working population, the essential point is that the peripheral workers occupy a subordinate position. How does it come about that a society can become divided in this fundamental way? Does such a division persist? What is its relation to other aspects of the society? What is its impact upon the economy itself?

The circumstances of the United States in the last decades of the nineteenth century encouraged whatever tendency may have existed in earlier American experience for individuals from distinct groups of the population to find themselves in a subordinate position in the labor markets. Sudden increases in the numbers of immigrants, and radical changes in their national origin, in their social, religious, and educational background, combined to create two distinct groups of workers. One group considered itself to be the true possessor of America, really "American" by virtue of its connection with a semi-mythical revolutionary and pioneering past, possessing some degree of education and skill, occupying positions of authority and influence, or tied by family to individuals who did.

The new immigrants were strange in tongue, in dress, in manner, and above all in religion to the dominant Protestant population of the northern cities. They were largely peasant in background, uneducated and equipped with skills more or less irrelevant to the urban industrial and commercial environment into which they were poured by the channels of immigration. Forced by their initial lack of capital into the most disorganized parts of the cities, they were impelled to accept whatever employment an economy engaged in a tremendous expansion of activity might offer them.

And employment this boisterous economy did offer them, but on its own terms. Their employment experience was fitful, casual, rough, and demoralizing. In boom years it was connected with the sudden expansion of construction activity, the building of cities and roads, mining, and lumbering. The flow of immigrants was, during these decades, a very sensitive register of the ups and downs of the economy. Even when there were sufficient employment opportunities to make immigration seem attractive to the European peasant, the kinds of work experience available to him often tended to lack continuity. He was still confined to those tasks at the bottom of the occupational and industrial hierarchy which were most peripheral, which lacked status. The recent immigrant was apt to have very little proprietarial interest in his job, he was not welcome in the craft unions, his relation to labor markets was in many cases mediated by the *padrone*, he was frequently part of a labor gang, anonymous himself, subject to arbitrary hiring and firing.

His position was indeed anomalous. According to the political norms of American society, he was, if not yet a citizen, potentially eligible for citizenship, and that in no great span of time. In a formal political sense, therefore, it seemed both to him and to the native-born American citizen that the expanding nation was opening its arms to him. The reality of political power was another matter. But it was possible for the dominant white Protestant majority to say to itself and to the immigrant, "What else can we be expected to do for you? We have already made the priceless gift of American citizenship to you. If you cannot make of it what we have ourselves been able to accomplish in spite of all the hardships of pioneering, you merely prove your inferiority." A popular and seemingly scientific literature, an outgrowth of nineteenth-century Darwinism, furnished support for this opinion.

Oscar Handlin has provided a graphic picture of the social exclusion of the "new immigrants" during the last decades of the nineteenth century and the early decades of the twentieth century, an exclusion whose increasing intensity led to the actual legal exclusion of further immigrants at the end of World War I.[1] This pervasive and powerful social exclusion, combined with nominal political acceptance, provided the basis for a profound ambivalence in American attitudes toward the immigrant population and their immediate descendants.

Politically the immigrant was "accepted" according to the fundamental law of the land, the idealized Constitution itself. Although a growing movement might advocate the prevention of more immigrants landing on American shores, no serious political movement advocated the denial of citizenship to immigrants as a matter of principle. It was expected that the immigrant would make some effort to Americanize himself by learning the rudiments of English and by mastering the elements of American history and showing acquaintance with the forms of American political processes. Socially, however, the immigrant was "unacceptable" unless his national background conformed to that of the dominant white Protestant group; unless he was a member of one of the numerous acceptable Protestant sects; unless his economic and educational achievements placed him within the middle class.

The consequences of this double view were bound to be very ramified. On the one hand, the dominant white Protestant group could feel, with a satisfactory degree of self-righteousness, that they had done all that could be expected of them, that the "new immigrant" was free to take his place in American life, that indeed the "new immigrant" had been treated with matchless generosity. In a political sense the illusion of community, of a shared political life, could be maintained. The ballot box made no distinctions. Any man could become president, except for the immigrant, and even the immigrant's son

[1] See Oscar Handlin, *The Uprooted* (Boston: Little, Brown and Company, 1951) and *Race and Nationality in American Life* (Boston: Little, Brown and Company, 1957).

could aspire that high. On the other hand, the "new immigrant" did not and could not, except in the rarest cases, really belong socially to the central core of the traditional American society. In a striking way, the political and social situation of the "new immigrant" in the United States represented a reversal of his age-old position in Europe. In Europe, he had been a socially full-fledged member of a highly organized community, the peasant village.

Unfortunately for the "new immigrant," a precedent for exclusion of a major portion of the society had long existed in American life. The Negro had been almost totally excluded, politically and socially, until the Civil War. During the very time that the "new immigrant" was arriving in ever increasing numbers, the Negro in the South was being systematically stripped of whatever formal political equality he had received as a result of that war. It was not difficult to find a rationale for the *de facto* subjection of the Negro. The Negro, and along with him the American Indian, and for good measure the Chinese and Japanese, were, it was asserted, racially inferior, morally and intellectually below the standards of American life. The proof of this inferiority was their poverty, their different standards of living, and their ignorance.

For the Negro, exclusion meant an almost absolute lack of access to any of the protections offered by federal or state governments, protections which in any case were apt to be particularly weak in the area of economic hazards. In a profound sense the nation learned "to look the other way," learned how "not to see" the Negro. It was all too easy to generalize this mental trait. For Negro one could partially substitute Southern European. If it was difficult to exclude the immigrant directly from the political community, it was all the more important that the immigrant not be included within the social community. His poverty, his place of residence, above all his lack of status within the occupational and industrial hierarchy made it almost certain that the average member of the white Protestant community would not think of him as one of "us" when it came to the question of the nature of his employment experience. Peripheral socially in a society where occupational status was of ever increasing importance, where it was expected that the full-fledged member of society would rise in the occupational hierarchy and have increasingly strong proprietarial interest in his job as he progressed through life, those immigrants who lacked any special attributes of cultural background, intellect, skill, capital, or just plain luck were forced to accept a most uncertain relationship to the world of work. They constituted the bulk of the peripheral labor force of the late nineteenth and early twentieth centuries. More important for the long run, the mainstream of American society developed deep-seated attitudes toward the kind of person who carried out the peripheral tasks of the economy, the casual day laborer, the intermittent worker, the part-time worker, attitudes which were destined to be carried over to those groups who succeeded the immigrant once the major flows of European and Asiatic immigration had ceased.

Basically such attitudes asserted, first, that it was right and proper that the peripheral work that the economy needed to have performed should be done by those demographic groups who occupied, in one critical sense or another, a subordinate position. Second, these attitudes made it possible for government to neglect to give the peripheral workers, drawn from these "inferior" groups, the same protection that a highly elaborate public and private apparatus, developing over these same years, came to afford the full-time, full-year nucleus of the American labor force.

In a society where to be an immigrant was to occupy an inferior and insecure position in the labor markets, it was only natural that the immigrant and his descendants would struggle to create institutions which could provide the security that

American society failed to afford. The immigrant came, for the most part, from European and Asiatic societies where very powerful and ancient institutions had operated to provide him with a secure role. Whether through the instrumentality of the village, the extended family, or the church, the individual could expect that the community into which he was born would afford him much the same status it afforded to any other member of his community similarly placed. While he was a youth, his work would be part of the training which a traditional society had developed to ensure that the village economy could continue from generation to generation. But his labor would also be a necessary part of the year's economic effort and would fit into the village economy in a meaningful way. For a girl, her training would fit her for the role of wife and mother, the combination of which would be more than enough to occupy her hours when she entered adulthood. As adult strength gave way to the feebleness of age, both men and women remained within the shelter of the community, although there seems to be some evidence that serious strains might develop over their role. It is worth noting, for instance, that even in the peasant villages of Eastern Europe it was not unusual in the nineteenth century for a village, hard pressed economically, to send its aged out as beggars. In addition, it seems to have been the rule that excess sons and daughters could not expect to be included within the community after they had reached adulthood.

As Handlin points out, the European peasant who emigrated to America was subject to the violent shock of leaving forever the protective, if collapsing, peasant community of Europe to enter a society which offered him none of this sense of community. He responded by trying to create his own institutions: mutual aid societies, burial societies, newspapers, churches, and so forth. One institution which he might have expected to offer him assistance, the trade union, did not. Only when he could make a trade union his own could he expect that it would act in his interest.

The history of nineteenth- and early twentieth-century American trade unions is filled with numberless incidents of exclusionary acts by the skilled craft unions, sometimes aimed at the skilled or semiskilled Negro worker, more generally aimed at the unskilled European and Asiatic immigrant. Indeed, the movement to end immigration found some of its strongest supporters among trade unionists. For several generations the American skilled worker was systematically taught by the majority of craft unions that the unskilled worker, flowing into the great urban centers in great numbers, was his enemy, a threat to his wage standards and his working conditions.

When in the course of time the children and grandchildren of immigrants entered the labor markets, no longer carrying with them the stigma of foreign tongue, foreign dress, foreign manners, now equal or superior to the average American in educational attainment, the barriers that their fathers and grandfathers had met at the entryway to the trade union were significantly lower for them. This was true even in the case of the old craft unions, many of which indeed were to become captives of particular ethnic groups. With the growth of the industrial trade unions, particularly since their period of most rapid growth came at a time of enormous crisis in the 1930s when unemployment was so universal that the traditional boundaries between the various demographic and occupational groups that comprised the American labor force tended to break down before a sense of common danger and shared disaster, many of the native-born descendants of the "new immigrants" found a strong shelter.

The lesson that their fathers' experience passed on to them was starkly simple. The fundamental function of a workers' institution must be to provide status. It must define the boundary between those who have a stake in the society and the outsider. Wages are important, it is true, but the measure of the success of a trade union can never be simply its ability to raise wages. Above all, a trade union exists to try to prevent its members from being treated as if they are peripheral.

It is something of a curiosity in the intellectual history of modern times that, in order to convict the trade movement in general of ineffectiveness, it was enough for some economists whose interests have centered upon the price system to show that it was impossible for the trade union movement as a whole to have had any very large effect upon general wage levels. But this is to impose middle-class values upon working-class institutions. To the average university professor it may indeed be true that the test of the success of an institution representing him would be its power to raise his income, particularly if his status is defined by academic tenure. But the very thing which the professors' institutions need do very little about, tenure and status, the working class institutions may be in a position to affect in highly significant ways. An employer may be quite unwilling to raise wages, particularly above the industry level, but he may be quite willing to change hiring and firing practices to provide greater security to the worker, particularly if the union can provide him with workers whose average productivity is higher than what an unstructured labor market could provide him and if the provision of security has a favorable effect upon the morale of his workers. Until we are quite clear in our minds about what it is that the worker wants, it seems fruitless to test the success of an institution by what might be an irrelevant goal. A proper test of the efficacy of aspirin is not how well it takes care of our stomach aches!

Soon after the rise of the powerful industrial unions the American economy entered a period of unprecedented expansion and low levels of unemployment. From the beginning of World War II until the present it has been possible for the nucleus of the labor force, the white married males, to expect something very close to full-time, full-year employment experience. Workers in particular industries and occupations have on occasion been an exception to this generalization, but it fits the year-in, year-out employment experience of the vast majority of white married males. This does not mean that there have not been episodes of interrupted employment in the lives of the typical members of this demographic group. Workers continue to shift from job to job and to experience occasional layoffs. Some occupational groups, such as construction workers and sales workers, continue to have markedly intermittent employment experience. The generalization does not assert the absence of occupational and industrial mobility. Rather it says that the typical white married male has achieved a considerable degree of status which provides him with the expectation of continuity of employment if he so desires. In some cases the status is derived from the power of his union. In other cases, particularly for the white-collar worker, it is derived from the character of the large-scale industrial and commercial bureaucracy which demands continuity of office (and personnel) where possible.

But the total functioning of the economic system also demands that work be performed at odd times, that a certain degree of flexibility in production and distribution be maintained. Indeed, flexibility in market output tends to increase if the share of personal services does.[2] Part-time and intermittent employment on a significant scale are inherent characteristics of dynamic economies and economies in which personal services constitute an important part of final demand. Where the climate imposes a strong seasonal character on production and demand, part-time and intermittent employment are even more an inherent characteristic.

When in the 1920s the great flow of white immigrants from Europe came to an abrupt end and the overwhelming majority

[2] I am indebted to Arnold Katz for this observation.

of white married males became full-time and full-year workers, the source of peripheral workers underwent a major
change. With the European and Asiatic immigrant no longer
available, other demographic groups filled the gap. Women,
youth, older workers, and minority groups such as the nonwhite, the Puerto Rican, and the Mexican increasingly came to
constitute the bulk of the peripheral labor force. It goes without saying that members of each of these groups are easily
identified and carry with them socially defined marks of their
"inferior" status.

In a sense the basic drama continued to be enacted, the only
change being in the cast. Other demographic groups upon
whom society could ascribe a label of innate inferiority simply
took the place of the immigrant. The basic attitudes of society
toward the peripheral worker did not need to be altered. It
remained proper that irregular, casual, part-time, intermittent
work should be performed by the "outsider." The "outsider"
was by definition biologically inferior (note that each group—
youth, women, older workers, Negroes, Puerto Ricans, Mexi-
cans—could be considered to labor under physical or racial
handicaps). Since the peripheral work of society was still
being performed by those who were not considered full-
fledged members of the labor force, it was not necessary to
ask, as it had not been necessary to ask in the case of the
immigrant, whether the peripheral worker was bearing too
large a share of the cost of the flexibility in work schedules
that the economy required.

As a result of this historical process the American labor
force became radically bifurcated. The boundaries of this
bifurcation between full-time, full-year workers and peripheral workers came to be lines of profound social cleavages
where primarily age, sex, and race characteristics (related to
national origin in the case of the Puerto Rican and Mexican)
were used as the markers for membership in one social cate-

gory or the other. Other markers, such as alcoholism, homosexuality, or criminal record, were used on occasion. It is important to note that the boundaries thus set up are not absolute barriers to movement between the peripheral labor force and the central nucleus of full-time, full-year workers. The barriers do not receive any legal sanction, nor does our explicit ideology support them. Rather they are like a tangle of thickets which can be traversed only by a combination of perserverance, favorable circumstances, and knowledge of the hidden paths. In the case of two groups, youth and the elderly, the barriers, being a function of age, will change with changing age. But the fact that the typical white male youth can, for example, expect in time to become a member of the full-time, full-year labor force does not lessen his peripheral status while he is still a youth. And our thesis maintains, essentially, that his status in the American economy is in several profound respects different from the status of youth in other highly developed economies, such as the European and Japanese.

An example may indicate the importance and some of the ramifications of this distinction between the work status of American and European youth. It has been a characteristic of European societies that it is difficult to alter the relatively early school-leaving age that characterizes even the most advanced of European countries. Freeing youth from work until the age of eighteen or more, particularly if the youth comes from a working-class background, seems a most radical step in these societies. But underlying such attitudes (not always shared by the working class itself) is a belief that it is in the middle and late teens that youth, through apprenticeship and other means, is brought into the labor force. In other words, even though European youth may not work the full schedules that the adult European works, he is treated as if he were in a probationary state during late adolescence. It is considered to be a matter of great social consequence that he receive training in adult skills and that these years of late adolescence be used to inculcate the proper commitment to work. An acceptance of the American pattern of education would involve a change in these patterns of socialization and therefore seems threatening. In the United States the work experience of youth is usually peripheral and a prolongation of education constitutes no threat, particularly since in a highly differentiated society the task of inculcating a proper adult sense of commitment to work is in fact not primarily the task of the economy.

In essence, the structure of the modern labor force, as sketched here, consists of a large nucleus of full-time, full-year workers, generally but not always employed by large-scale organizations. This nucleus possesses a considerable amount of "status" and is protected by a host of private and public institutions. Surrounding it is a group of "peripheral workers," numbering many millions, who do not have the status and protection taken for granted by workers who from one year to the next are likely to have continuous full-time employment.

How does this conception of the development of the structure of the American labor force compare with older views? The source of most nineteenth-century English conceptions of the labor force is Adam Smith's *Wealth of Nations*. Smith's treatment of labor (and wages) has several interesting features from our point of view. The problem of wages is divided into two parts. There is first of all an analysis of the "natural price" and the "market price" of labor in which labor is treated more or less as if it were homogeneous. Workers are the "labouring poor," "the servants labourers and workmen of different kinds [who] make up the far greater part of every political society." [3] Later Smith takes up another question, that of wage differentials. His approach is comprehensive but rests upon the

[3] Adam Smith, *The Wealth of Nations*, Modern Library Edition (New York: Random House, 1937), p. 78.

implicit assumption that wage differentials arise almost entirely
"from certain circumstances in the employments themselves,"
rather than from inherent differences in workers. Labor is
treated still as if it were by nature homogeneous. There is, says
Smith, less difference between the philosopher and the porter
"in genius and disposition" than between the mastiff and the
greyhound.[4] Smith maintains that "the differences of natural
talents in different men is, in reality, much less than we are
aware of; and the very different genius which appears to distinguish men of different professions . . . is not upon many
occasions so much the cause, as the effect of the division of
labour." [5] With a few exceptions, wage differentials represent
compensation either for the increased cost of particular occupations (particularly training costs) or for the unusual severity or unpleasantness of particular "employments." These
differentials are added to the wages of common labor, the basic
wage from which all other wages are derived, so that the "net
advantages" of all employments will always remain equal. The
"net advantages" must be equal, Smith maintains, because the
labor market is free and competitive.

The model of the labor market that emerges from Smith's
chapters on wages and his incidental comments on human
nature has several basic elements. First, labor is inherently
homogeneous (or at least more nearly homogeneous than people think); second, the labor market is competitive and free;
third, different "employments" have differing degrees of hardship, unpleasantness, skill, trust, continuity, and probability of
success, and differential wage rates must compensate for these
differences. Finally, the quantity of labor demanded and the
quantity supplied are equated by the "market price," but at
the same time lags in the movement of the basic wage rate lead
to temporary imbalance between the quantity of labor demanded and the quantity supplied. During such periods unem-

<hr />

[4] *Ibid.*, p. 16.   [5] *Ibid.*, p. 15.

ployment can arise, this unemployment being more or less randomly distributed among the working population.

The "industriousness" of a population, which in the context seems to mean both the proportion of the population that is in the labor force *and* the hours of work, is determined by whether, in Smith's sense of the term, the demand is for "productive" or "unproductive" labor.

We are more industrious than our forefathers; because in the present times the funds destined for the maintenance of industry, are much greater in proportion to those which are likely to be employed in the maintenance of idleness, than they were two or three centuries ago. Our ancestors were idle for want of a sufficient encouragement to industry. It is better, says the proverb, to play for nothing, than to work for nothing. In mercantile and manufacturing towns, where the inferior ranks of people are chiefly maintained by the employment of capital, they are in general industrious, sober, and thriving; as in many English and in most Dutch towns. In those towns which are principally supported by the constant or occasional residence of a court, and in which the inferior ranks of people are chiefly maintained by the spending of revenue, they are in general idle, dissolute and poor; as at Rome, Versailles, Compienne and Fontainebleu. If you except Rouen and Bordeaux, there is little trade or industry in any of the paraliament towns of France; and the inferior ranks of people, being chiefly maintained by the expense of the members of the courts of justice . . . are in general idle and poor. . . . The proportion between capital and revenue, therefore, seems everywhere to regulate the proportion between industry and idleness.[6]

The distinction between capital and revenue here is roughly the distinction between "manufacturing" and "commerce" on the one hand and "services" on the other, particularly domestic service. Smith was strongly impressed by the higher degree of "peripherality" in the "service" sector of the economy of his time.

Marx developed a somewhat more elaborate version of the

[6] *Ibid.*, pp. 319–21.

classical theory and his interpretation has some topical interest today. In the Marxist system, a constant pool of unemployed workers is an essential element. This pool, the "industrial reserve army," is recruited from several sources. The employers are always under pressure to substitute capital for labor. The effect of technological progress is to heighten this pressure. The demand for labor, therefore, tends constantly to decrease and wages to fall to or below the subsistence level (hence Marx's theory of increasing immiserization of the working class). Since wages are, however, somewhat sticky at the subsistence level, part of the labor force tends to be unemployed. From our point of view, there is an interesting subsidiary point to Marx's position. Those workers who are subject to unemployment over very long periods finally become demoralized and withdraw from the labor force entirely to form the *lumpenproletariat*. Marx assumes, however, that the vast body of the working class (the *lumpenproletariat* is never considered to form a very large body) is subject to intermittent rather than permanent unemployment.

As Marx views the economy, the vast bulk of workers have no status, no security in their employment. Unemployment is rotated among them. Labor is relatively homogeneous, workers who are presently unemployed eventually secure employment, those who are employed are eventually displaced in their turn by capital and technological progress.

But there are other elements in the situation of capitalist economies which, in the Marxist view, tend to make employment a fitful, intermittent, insecure condition. In the first place, such economies are subject to violent periodic crises; secondly, the process of capital accumulation destroys the smaller and less powerful firms; and, finally, the unplanned character of capitalist production leads to all sorts of partial "gluts," signaling abrupt cutbacks of output when the glut is finally recognized. The effect of all these elements is more or less random as far as the employment prospects of any individual worker are concerned. There is no necessary tendency for one particular group of workers to suffer more severe unemployment than other groups. The working class is "all in it together," and it is in part because all workers are equally subject to unemployment that a sense of class solidarity eventually emerges. No privileged group of workers can expect to be protected against the hardships of periodic unemployment for very long.

While Marx was developing this model of the labor market under capitalist conditions, another, and rather different, kind of analysis of the labor market was being formulated by John Stuart Mill. Mill was willing to entertain the possibility that in the modern industrial competitive economies some prices, among them wages, might be customary in character, rather than determined by supply and demand in competitive markets. The labor market itself, he felt, was made up of a number of groups which were in important respects noncompeting.[7] In other words, instead of one single labor market, the economy possessed a number of separate labor markets. The boundaries (or rather the barriers) between these markets were fundamentally social in character. Finally, Mill held that the workers could, by coming together, change their individual situations and even alter the character of the economy itself. Workers, in other words, had the power to change their status in fundamental ways, and were fast learning, as the example of trade unions and the French cooperatives showed, how to use this power. Mill, with his customary balance of optimism and pessimism, noted that there was some danger that the upper strata of the working class might use their greater ability in order to organize for parochial rather than

[7] This view was not restricted to Mill. It occupies a prominent place in J. E. Cairne's analysis of the condition of labor.

societal purposes, creating in the process a deep cleavage in the working class as a whole.

Since Mill's day the concept of noncompeting groups in one form or another has appeared in much of the literature dealing with wages. Alfred Marshall, for example, devoted some attention to noncompeting groups in the chapters in the *Principles* which deal with wages. He emphasized the distinction between horizontal and vertical mobility. A relatively high degree of horizontal mobility ensured that workers on the same social level received much the same remuneration, no matter where they worked or what labor they performed. Society, however, was composed of a number of distinct social levels and between these levels there was relatively little mobility; hence gaps in wage rates between one social level and another could develop. Moreover, as we noted in Chapter II, Marshall was very much concerned about the status of the lowest group, the residuum, whose condition tended to deteriorate from one generation to another. There was, believed Marshall, very little chance that this lowest stratum of society could improve its lot through its own unaided efforts. Like Mill, Marshall was persuaded that the condition of the lowest levels of society could be transformed only by a very abrupt and radical change in their environment, of sufficient scope and duration to permit the development of permanently higher aspirations and new living habits.

Since Marshall's time, the emphasis of economists dealing with labor has been largely on such questions as the determination of relative wage rates and aggregate employment levels. In recent years labor force participation rates have been another important area of interest. However, relatively little attention has been paid to the determinants of the distribution of part-time and/or intermittent employment experience until quite recently.

If we abandon the view that part-time and intermittent employment experience is more or less randomly distributed among the working population, then we are forced to come to grips with several distinct but closely related questions. First of all, we must ask what the influences are which, singly or together, lead to a particular demographic or social group contributing a more than proportionate share of either part-time or intermittent work experience.

Related to the question of whether particular demographic groups and social classes tend to constitute the bulk of the peripheral labor force is the question of whether particular industries and occupations tend to use a conspicuously higher proportion of peripheral workers than other industries and occupations. If so, do these industries and occupations share common features, such as size of the typical firm or degree of training and education which the employee is expected to have and extent of training and education which the firm usually supplies? Where is peripheral work usually located? Is it found more often in rural environments? Does it cluster in the older large cities?

THE SOCIOLOGY OF
PERIPHERAL WORK EXPERIENCE

PERIPHERALITY AND SOCIAL STATUS

The first part of this chapter has presented a thesis about the peripheral worker in American society which is explicitly historical and partly sociological in character. In essence, the thesis asserts several interrelated propositions:

(1) It is possible to rank demographic groups in American society by social status.

(2) It is possible to rank occupations (and, to some extent, industries) by status.

(3) In general, low status occupations (and industries, to some extent) have been and at present are associated with demographic groups who possess low social status. Indeed, the link between the status of a demographic group and an occupation may be much more intimate than this statement indicates. If an occupation has traditionally been one of low status, then it confers low status upon the individuals or groups who are involved in it. Conversely, the presence of social groups of low status in a particular occupation tends to confer low status on that occupation. The resistance presented by individuals of groups of high social status to the entry of individuals of low status into previously high status occupations is undoubtedly in large part due to the fear that low status will be transferred from the social group to the occupation. This seems to be a very general anxiety, felt most strongly perhaps by just those groups which have most recently achieved some degree of status.

(4) The status of an occupation (and of industries) is in part a function of the continuity of employment it affords.

(5) Occupations (and industries) which have least continuity of employment will therefore be filled, in general, by those demographic groups possessing least social status.

(6) Social status in American life is conferred by, among many other attributes, (a) sex, (b) age, (c) color, and (d) national origin. When immigration was on a large scale, date of arrival in America was an important determinant of status. Other things being equal, social status was determined by the number of generations of American-born ancestors an individual possessed. A marked decrease in social status occurred when both parents were foreign-born, particularly when the country of origin was itself associated with low status. When an individual was actually an immigrant from countries of low status, he was ranked at the bottom of the status scale.

The conclusion that follows from these propositions is that

peripheral work experience, inherently less continuous than other types of work experience, is therefore a characteristic of demographic groups whose sex, age, or color assign to them low status. In contemporary America these groups are (1) females, (2) younger and older workers, and (3) the nonwhite.

THE PROCESS OF COMMITMENT TO WORK

Another way of looking at the peripheral labor force centers upon the process of commitment to work, to occupation, and to industry. This approach considers commitment to work to be the outcome of a lengthy and multistage process in which two institutions, the family and the school, not ordinarily considered to be part of the economy as such, are of strategic importance.[8]

Fundamental attitudes toward work are initially formed within the family. These attitudes are reinforced and made more specific in school. If the process of commitment has developed smoothly, the young adult enters the labor force with a set of values which permit the succeeding stages of commitment to take place without difficulty. These later stages are located entirely within the economy proper and involve the eventual assignment of the adult worker to a specific task within a particular organization.

This approach to the matter, centering on the process of commitment to work, would consider the peripheral work experience of young workers to be in large part the result of the incomplete development of their commitment to work. The young worker is in the labor force, but commitment to a specific occupation or industry can take place only *within* the economy itself and necessarily these stages of commitment

[8] This section is much indebted to the views of Talcott Parsons and Neal Smelser in *Economy and Society* (New York: The Free Press, 1956). See particularly their analysis of the process of labor commitment in Chapter II.

take time. The young worker *cannot*, in the normal process of commitment, enter the labor force with a complete commitment to a specific occupation and industry, and in any case his commitment and assignment to a specific task within a particular employing institution awaits his arrival at this employing institution and its assessment of his capabilities.

The character of peripheral work experience of older workers, on the other hand, is shaped by the fact that the older worker must give up commitments to specific jobs. In the usual case the abandonment of these commitments leads to anxiety and confusion. The situation is complicated by compulsory retirement requirements, private and public pension plans, and seniority provisions of union contracts which tend to "lock" an older worker into his job but also tend to make it more difficult for an older worker to find employment if he chances to become unemployed. Complex institutional constraints upon work experience of older workers, along with the fact that only in the last few decades have life expectancies reached a point where the average male worker can expect to live a number of years after he has stopped working, make it very difficult to say what would be the patterns of work experience of the older worker if the physiological and psychological impacts of aging were the only factors altering his earlier patterns of commitment to work. (Life expectancy for white males aged 20 in the United States in 1900 was only 42.19 years. As late as 1940, life expectancy for this group was still only 47.76 years.)

For the two other demographic groups who have differentially high rates of peripheral work experience, women and nonwhites, the explanation may lie in what happens in two different early stages of the total process of commitment to work. Since full commitment to work is a complex resultant of a number of separate stages, reaching far back into childhood, it may be that the answer to lack of full adult commitment, manifesting itself in peripheral work experience, is really located in early childhood, in the family or in school. The male white child may typically be exposed to strong influences which induce a positive set toward full-time adult work experience. ("When I grow up I'm going to be a fireman.") In his case the typical parent-son relationship encourages the development of attitudes favorable to the eventual assumption of responsibility for self-support and for the formation of future families in which the male will work full time to provide the major part of the family income. To the extent that the personality formation of the male child rests upon identification with the male parent, the very fact that in the overwhelming majority of cases this parent is a full-time worker if the child is white tends to create a self-image in the child which includes commitment to work as one of the highest of values.

School experience reinforces these early childhood influences in powerful and pervasive ways. Homework is designed to teach the child to apply himself to unpleasant tasks, to respond to a system of rewards and punishments. The adolescent male child comes to expect that the end of his schooling means the beginning of his adult life of work. If school affords him only minimal achievement and satisfaction, he comes to look forward to the day when he will be done with school and free to work. If, on the contrary, he is relatively successful at school, he has already responded to the system of rewards which it offers and which lead him through college into the world of work in which his expectations of secure well-paid employment are high.

For the typical female child, however, both early childhood and school influences do not encourage the formation of positive commitment to eventual full-time work experience. Rather the female child tends to develop highly ambivalent attitudes toward work. Adult work may be seen as punishment for failure to be sufficiently feminine to get married or to stay married. Youthful consumption patterns reinforce attitudes toward work. The toys of the male child tend to be "work toys," his adolescent activities center around images of masculine work—making and repairing cars, building models, making electronic equipment. For the girl, the emphasis is upon "home centered" toys, upon the development of skills as a consumer and homemaker. The dump truck and the doll's house are profound cultural symbols, prefiguring in imagination the child's expected adult role. School experiences, too, lead the typical girl to ambivalent attitudes toward work. Quite aside from the home economics courses and the pervasive attitudes, expressed by students and teachers alike, that mathematics and science courses are "masculine" and the foundation for later careers, major nonacademic activities in school, particularly in high school, center around sports in which hard work leads to success, in which "team spirit" is inculcated as part of the preparation of the adolescent boy for the kind of cooperative work activity which he will be engaged in as an adult. The figure of the girl cheerleader could hardly better symbolize the "peripheral" quality of the adolescent girl in the masculine world of effort, pain, achievement, and failure.

For many nonwhite children what has been said about girls applies with redoubled force, whether the nonwhite child is male or female. In particular, the situation of the nonwhite male child is frequently adverse to the development of early stages of commitment to work. A much larger proportion of nonwhite boys than of white boys grow up from their first years without a male adult in their immediate environment who can provide a model of, and the stimulus to, full commitment to a successful career of adult work. Indeed, it is often the woman who has the more stable and successful work career. If the male adult in the nonwhite child's life does work full time, it is all too often in a dead-end occupation, an occupation which the adult male feels to be both poorly rewarded and degrading. If the environment is rural, the young non-white male child sees the work of his parents as an aspect of a collapsing system of agriculture in which failure and exclusion from the world of work often have seemed to be the reward for grinding years of labor. If the environment of the non-white child is urban, one of its major features may be a pervasive instability of residence and school. An ordered set of relationships with neighbors, community, church, and school is hard to come by. In particular, adolescent school experiences may be strongly adverse to the development of positive attitudes toward work. The nonwhite male adolescent does not usually take an academic course designed to prepare him for college, while the commercial high schools and the trade schools often seem to him to be mere holding operations. From his point of view they are not really preparing him for the kind of work which he feels lies in wait for him.

If he does obtain a high school diploma, he may nevertheless have grave doubts about the quality of his education, doubts which do not encourage him to apply for jobs which require the use of this education. If he drops out of school, he is told that he has forfeited the possibility of—almost the right to—jobs which will have any status. Moreover, if he drops out of school, he is so young that the labor market automatically excludes him from serious consideration for full-time, full-year jobs, even when they require a minimum of skill and experience. He is therefore fated to undergo a long series of highly peripheral work experiences, if he is to have any work experience at all. It is clear, therefore, that for a sizable group of nonwhite male youth the process of commitment to work has been so undermined by early and late childhood experience that a fairly likely outcome is a loose attachment to the labor force or eventual nonparticipation in the labor market at all.

THE ECONOMICS OF
PERIPHERAL WORK EXPERIENCE

PERIPHERALITY AND CHANGING PATTERNS
OF SEASONALITY

Intermittent employment, by and large, has historically been associated with seasonality, which necessarily produced a large amount of such employment experience in the past. On the one hand, there were the seasonal fluctuations in employment levels which were the direct result of the climatic round of the year. In economies largely agricultural in character, much of the seasonal variation in employment tended to take the form of outright idleness, higher frequency of feast days in slack seasons, or performance of tasks which could be postponed to the off-seasons. Rural handicrafts might also develop, characterized in many instances by very low earnings, reflecting the low marginal productivity of the agricultural worker in his principal occupation, farming, during off-seasons. In an economic sense, handicraft occupations might be considered simply to be a form of disguised underemployment to the extent that earnings in them were conspicuously below earnings in occupations requiring similar skills and aptitudes. On the other hand, these alternative and intermittent opportunities to earn at least some income during the off-seasons made it possible for the earnings of many agriculturalists during the agricultural seasons of the year to be somewhat below what they would have been if the market for handicrafts produced during the off-seasons had not developed.

Seasonal fluctuations of employment in construction activity and in transportation were also extremely severe up to the fairly recent past. One of the major influences of the railroad and the steamboat was to decrease to a very great degree the dependence of land and water transportation operations upon tolerable weather conditions. Moreover, since these new forms of transportation, involving very large aggregations of fixed capital, operated on fixed schedules which could be maintained except under the most adverse weather conditions, it was less necessary to have as large a pool of casual labor attached to the transportation industries.

To the extent that in the past a large part of construction activity had to take place at the site itself and could not be carried on in unseasonable weather, the construction industry was also in the grip of the seasons. One of the major shifts in this industry has taken the form of the development of techniques which make it possible to employ a good part of the labor inputs which ultimately will go into the finished structure in offsite locations protected against inclement weather. Prefabricated plumbing and prefabricated electrical installations are merely the latest of such developments. At earlier periods precut siding, precut lumber, prefabricated window and door frames all testified to the continual substitution of activity which could be carried out the year round in protected structures for the type of activity which earlier had taken place at the site itself.

As the relative importance of agriculture decreased in the more advanced economies, the importance of seasonal factors in creating intermittent employment may have tended to decrease for the economy as a whole. However, another type of seasonal influence, only in part climatic, has become of increasing importance in some sectors of the economy. Demand for consumer goods, both durable and nondurable, has tended to show marked seasonality, on the one hand associated with major holidays, on the other with model and style changes. And as the economy becomes more and more dominated by services, those services which of necessity are related to seasons tend to replace older types of productive activity which were dominated by seasonal factors. Tourism, along with associated activities, is perhaps the most clear-cut example of a service industry showing marked seasonality, but it should be noted that education has traditionally been seasonal in its operation and its increasing relative importance adds somewhat to the total seasonality of employment.

Intermittent employment, then, can be due to seasonal factors impinging on the side of supply, largely of a climatic character, and seasonal factors operating largely through seasonal patterns of fluctuating demand, in part climatic in character but in part the result of institutional factors such as annual model changes. This seasonally induced intermittent employment is more or less predictable and the workers that are affected by it can be expected to be largely of two types. On the one hand, there are those individuals—for example, women employed in seasonal food processing—who enter the labor force only when there is demand for their services in a seasonal industry. Their pattern of life includes intermittent employment of a specific type, occurring at predictable times and of predictable duration. For the remainder of the year they may be quite accustomed to remain out of the labor force and they may consider their intermittent employment to be entirely "voluntary" in character.

On the other hand, there are those individuals, typified, for example, by the migratory agricultural laborer, who try to piece together out of several periods of intermittent work for different employers and in different industries a pattern of employment for the entire year which comes as close as possible to full-year employment. Such workers may shift from one part of the country to another, but they may also, as in the apparel industries of New York City, shift from one branch of the industry to another as periods of peak demand for a particular type of labor shift

RANDOM FLUCTUATIONS

A very different type of peripheral worker whose work experience may be intermittently full time is the worker brought into the work force of a firm or an industry and dismissed according to relatively unpredictable shifts in the firm's or the industry's output. The output of almost any industry is liable to random variations originating both on the demand and on the supply side. In some cases it may be that the nature of the production processes themselves makes it desirable for the firm to operate either at full capacity or not at all. Some parts suppliers, for example, may find it more profitable to make large runs and then to shut down a department, preferring to place finished output in inventories rather than to operate on a small scale. Within a firm itself, part of the work force may be almost continually employed, the burden of variations in output falling almost entirely upon certain departments, occupations, or classes of workers. In general, the technical, managerial, and maintenance work force can expect full-year employment while the semiskilled blue-collar operatives are expected to be willing to accept variable work schedules—short days and short weeks—as the necessity for variation in output impinges upon the firm. Contractual arrangements between employer and employee tend to give such discrimination in hiring and dismissal practices some degree of status by dividing the work force into the salaried and nonsalaried, the implication being that the nonsalaried worker has no formal claim to continuity of employment.

The discussion of intermittent employment up to this point has been centered on the various factors which may make the demand for workers of a firm or an industry fluctuate in such a fashion that some groups of workers experience intermittent employment as a more or less chronic condition. The range of possible variation among firms, industries, and occupations is very wide. The economy as a whole, however, requires a total labor market which is sufficiently flexible so that it is possible to vary inputs of labor in differing sectors of the economy in bewilderingly complex fashion in order to meet seasonal and random fluctuations of output due to pressures originating either on the side of demand or on the side of supply. But firms and industries develop quite different institutional patterns to handle variable labor inputs. The traditional (but now rapidly disappearing) shape-up to be found in industries like longshoring is only one extreme; at the other pole it is possible to find collective bargaining agreements which purport to guarantee full-year employment, or at least an approximation of full-year employment. Industries which in fact are characterized by considerable intermittency of employment, such as schoolteaching with its customary three-month vacation, may at the same time develop hiring practices which provide for security of employment during specified periods of the year.

Moreover, it is important to note that intermittency of employment takes place as much along an occupational axis as it does on a firm or industrial axis. For many occupations, particularly for some of the professions, one of the characteristics of the labor market may in fact be the camouflage it provides for high degrees of intermittency of actual employment, the impression given to the outsider being that the individual member is employed with much more continuity than he is in fact. Indeed, it is possible that Adam Smith's conjecture that there would be chronic underemployment in those professions where some individuals were very highly rewarded, because of the psychological propensity of young people to overestimate their chances of success, is still relevant to certain professions. Actors and musicians are perhaps spectacular examples today of the acuteness of Smith's insight.

Intermittent and part-time work experience is a pronounced characteristic of some sectors or subsectors of the economy and almost unknown in others. Certain types of economic organizations make extensive use of peripheral workers, others avoid using them. In general, bureaucratic firms, with high capital/labor ratios, employ primarily full-time, full-year employees. In such firms a significant part of labor costs has many of the features of fixed costs. Such firms are also apt to have market relations which differ in important respects from the small firm in a competitive industry. They are apt to be multiplant, multi-product nationwide firms. Individual plants are frequently located in communities which are small relative to the size of the plant so that the employment practices of the firm and the employment level maintained in the plant have noticeable effects upon the economic life of the entire community.

Robert Averitt has recently proposed that American industry is really composed of two types of firms—"center" firms and "periphery" firms.

The center firm is large in economic size as measured by number of employees, total assets, and yearly sales. It tends toward vertical integration (through ownership or informal control), geographic dispersion (national and international), product diversification, and managerial decentralization. . . . Center managements combine a long-run with a short-run perspective. . . .

The periphery firm is relatively small. It is not integrated vertically, and it may be an economic satellite of a center firm or cluster of center firms. Periphery firms are less geographically dispersed, both nationally and internationally. Typically they produce only a small line of related products. . . . Their emphasis is on short-run probems. . . . [They] usually inhabit relatively unconcentrated markets.[9]

[9] Robert Averitt, *The Dual Economy* (New York: W. W. Norton, 1968), pp. 1–2.

The distinction that Averitt draws between center and periphery firms is similar in verbal terms to the distinction we have drawn between the nucleus of the labor force (the full-time, full-year workers) and the peripheral labor force (the part-time and intermittent workers). Is there a very close correspondence between his periphery firm and our peripheral workers? Are the circumstances of the peripheral worker derived from the economic situation in which the periphery firm finds itself?

There is at least one sharp distinction between our use of the term "peripheral" and Averitt's use of the term. Averitt considers that the typical center firm is engaged in manufacturing. He has in mind firms like U.S. Steel and General Motors. Conglomerate firms like Textron and Lytton Industries are in his view prototypes of the center firm of the immediate future. In addition, the center firm includes firms engaged in mass retailing, like Sears Roebuck and A & P. All these firms, according to Averitt, "have significant influence over and knowledge of the major technical, political, and economic forces that determine their life chances." [10] On the other hand, the "defining quality of periphery firms is settled by *small size* and *limited potential*." [11] Limited potential in turn is derived from the behavior of the periphery firm's long-run cost, which must, beyond a relatively small level of output, "necessarily rise." Averitt's center firms, therefore, are generally oligopolistic; periphery firms tend to be competitive.

Our distinction between the full-time, full-year nucleus of the labor force and the peripheral worker emphasizes the fact that differing sectors of the economy use very different proportions of peripheral workers. Agriculture has always relied heavily upon intermittent and part-time workers, perhaps as much or more today than in the past. Many of the industries in the service sector also are characterized by a relatively high

[10] *Ibid.*, pp. 79–80.   [11] *Ibid.*, p. 87.

proportion of peripheral workers in their work forces. A number of occupations, as well as industries, have high proportions of peripheral workers.

On the other hand, it is likely that the oligopolistic firm does have a stable work force and that therefore what we have called the nucleus of the labor force, the full-time, full-year workers, is located disproportionately in such firms and therefore in the industries where such firms are typically found. However, it is also important to take account of the fact that total employment in firms which can properly be classified as oligopolistic industrial firms is not as large a fraction of total employment in the economy as one might think.

Moreover, within those sectors of the economy where large oligopolistic firms might be expected to be found, manufacturing, communication, and transportation, by no means all firms are properly classified as large scale and oligopolistic. In manufacturing alone, there were some 95,000 operating establishments in 1958 (each plant with 20 or more employees), employing a total of 15.4 million individuals, of whom 11.6 were production workers.[12]

In 1964 the five hundred largest industrial corporations (ranked by sales) in the United States employed only about 10.5 million people. When we recall that some forty-seven million individuals had full-time, full-year work experience during that year, while an additional 38 million individuals had part-year or part-time work experience, or some combination of both, it is clear that the nucleus of the work force is by no means coextensive with large-scale business organizations, Averitt's center firms. The peripheral worker, too, is not coextensive with Averitt's periphery firms. Indeed, as a later section of this chapter emphasizes, one characteristic of part of the work force of many small firms is a very strong attachment to the firm. At the same time, large firms do strive to

[12] *Statistical Abstract of the United States,* 1961, p. 781.

offer a high degree of continuity of employment, and it is evident that in many cases they come very close to approaching the goal of a stable work force. The increasing willingness of industry leaders to consider some form of guaranteed annual employment is a reflection of what has in many cases become a *de facto* situation. The emergence of a movement to place workers formerly paid by the hour on a monthly salary symbolizes a profound change in the employment status of many blue-collar workers.

In Chapter I it was pointed out that firms can be expected to attempt wherever possible to try to achieve relatively constant levels of output in any given plant. Indeed, one of the technological imperatives of the age seems to be a drive to approximate wherever possible a continuous-flow production process. In a world of certainty, a manufacturing plant should be designed for a constant flow of output, interrupted only rarely by maintenance requirements, wherever the scale of production and the state of technology make this possible. Installations of this type usually require very heavy investments of capital. Interruptions of production for whatever purpose entail heavy costs. Shut-down operations are complex, costs of capital are fixed, start-up operations are difficult. In fact, labor requirements are usually many times heavier at shut-down and start-up operations than during routine production.

Where a firm is not able to plan for constant levels of operations, where it must take into account an uncertain future, it will, as A. G. Hart has pointed out, build potential flexibility of output into its plant.[13] This flexibility can in general be attained, however, only by the firm's being willing to accept an average cost curve which is higher and at the same time flatter than that of a firm in a position to construct a plant designed for an unchanging level of output.

[13] Albert G. Hart, *Anticipation, Uncertainty, and Dynamic Planning* (Chicago: University of Chicago Press, 1940; reprinted, New York: A. M. Kelley, 1951).

Large firms, particularly multi-plant firms, can be expected to be pioneers in the introduction of continuous flow processes. If continuous flow is unobtainable over the whole range of the productive process, it is often possible to attain continuous flow operation in subsectors. For a number of reasons the large firm is in a particularly favorable position to introduce such technology. Even if total output is somewhat variable, the firm may find that it is possible to utilize at least one continuous flow plant because total demand for its product can seldom be expected to fall below the capacity of the continuous flow installation. If it is desirable to attain higher levels of output, the firm can utilize obsolescent facilities in its possession or, as frequently happens, subcontract with satellite firms. In addition, large firms can obtain capital on relatively favorable terms. Finally, the large firm is able to maintain a technical staff to keep it abreast of the latest technological possibilities and frequently to develop the requisite technology.

If the labor force necessary to operate intricate and costly continuous flow process plants must receive intensive, expensive, and specialized training, there is an additional incentive on the part of the firm to offer continuity of employment. Any layoff contains a considerable risk that a labor force assembled at great expense, with great difficulty, and over a long period of time will be dissipated to rivals, as a number of defense firms specializing in aviation and space technology have found to their very great cost.

Around large manufacturing firms a host of smaller firms will swarm, each offering to supply goods and services which are needed either in such small quantities that continuous flow operations are uneconomical or at uncertain times or in uncertain quantities. These small firms must use a technology which permits them to vary their output both in kind and in quantity. They in turn will rely heavily upon variable inputs of labor.

In this scheme of industrial organization, the large firm specializes in continuity of output and offers concomitant continuity of employment. Flexibility of output, an unavoidable necessity in a world of uncertainty, seasonality, catastrophe, and change of taste and technology, is to a disproportionate extent provided by smaller firms which specialize in meeting the costs of uncertainty and changing levels and types of output.

Up to this point the discussion has been centered on the manufacturing firm. In the interest of comprehensiveness we must note that there is one type of productive unit which may be less likely to feel the pressure to reduce costs by shifting the provision of flexibility to some other unit. It is, however, even more likely not to respond except in time of crisis to the costs of excessive inflexibility. This type of organization is the nonprofit producing unit—in particular, governmental agencies, but including the whole gamut of not-for-profit activity, the universities, nonprofit hospitals, and so forth. Ginzberg, Hiestand, and Reubens point out in *The Pluralistic Economy* that "not less than one-third and possibly two-fifths of all employment is accounted for by the activities of the not-for-profit sector." [14] Any analysis of the labor market which fails to take into account both the size of the not-for-profit sector and its special character runs the risk of being irrelevant to the employment experience of a major and increasing segment of the population. The statistical data that are currently being generated each month and each year about the labor force unfortunately do not make it possible to isolate easily or quickly the experience of that portion of the working population that has work experience in not-for-profit organizations.

One characteristic of such not-for-profit units is that their labor force frequently comes to believe that it possesses some-

[14] Eli Ginzberg, Dale Hiestand, and Beatrice Reubens, *The Pluralistic Economy* (New York: McGraw-Hill, 1965), p. 193.

thing like tenure, purchased in many cases, it may be, by means of relatively low remuneration.

If the total economy still requires a certain degree of flexibility and if the nonprofit sector tends to have an excessive degree of inflexibility, at least from the point of view of its labor inputs, then it might be expected that some other sector of the economy, or some other element in the labor force, or the consumer of the output of the not-for-profit sector himself may have to furnish a relatively larger amount of flexibility and its associated cost than would otherwise be the case.

The striking extent to which government office hours are not adjusted to meet the convenience of the consumer is evident to anyone who has had occasion to stand in line to secure a driver's license during the middle of the day. Large bureaucracies tend to develop uniform schedules of hours and it is often hard to bring to the attention of government officials the cost to the consumer of operating hours which are not adjusted to the schedules of users of government services.

VOLUNTARY AND INVOLUNTARY PERIPHERAL WORK

A question of very great interest (and of increasing importance) is whether intermittent and part-time employment is by and large imposed on a labor force whose members for the most part are desirous of working full-year, full-time schedules or whether, on the other hand, intermittent and part-time employment is largely the natural result of the desire of a considerable number of individuals to avoid what they may regard as an overcommitment to the world of work. It is possible to find copious illustrations of both situations. Intermittent layoffs, more or less as an accepted pattern, characterize some industries, and it would be difficult to maintain in many of these cases that the variability of income and the uncertainty that result are preferred by the great bulk of the employees. But it may very well be true that the intermittent employment found in the construction industry, to take one example, does represent a preferred pattern of activity for many of its members.

If, moreover, we think of occupations, rather than of firms or industries, it is possible to find several occupations where the preferred work experience of many individuals seems to be intermittent employment. Sales workers are a fairly conspicuous example, a more exotic example being the professional athlete. And it is probable that for a sizable fraction of the teaching profession one of the most attractive characteristics of their work experience is the pattern of vacations it offers.

Ideally, the desirable state of affairs would be one where the flexibility of the labor market and the variability of employment patterns among firms, industries, and occupations would provide sufficient scope both for those workers who desired continuity of employment and for those who desired intermittent employment. Indeed, a labor market characterized by a high degree of mobility and a high degree of knowledge of options would be expected to adjust the supply of those workers desiring intermittent employment of a particular type to the demand for such workers in large part through the agency of wage differentials between full-year and intermittent employment.

However, it seems impossible to determine *a priori* what forms these wage differentials would take, whether, that is, wages for full-year employment would or would not be, for any particular period of time one might specify, higher than wages for intermittent employment of comparable skill level and other characteristics. In the type of labor market we have in mind, where the worker is highly mobile and highly informed, there could not be a persistent group of workers who were dissatisfied with their work experience unless at the same time there was general and involuntary unemployment. It might be interesting to speculate about whether, under conditions of general unemployment, unemployment would bear more heavily upon workers desiring full-year employment than upon those willing to accept intermittent employment, but again it seems impossible to give a plausible *a priori* answer to this kind of question.

In an economy characterized by a flexible and informed labor market we can, however, conclude that an increase in the desire for intermittent employment experience relative to full-year employment would produce, via a shift in relative wage rates, a substitution of intermittent workers for full-year workers. It is also probable that one of the things that workers would wish to "purchase" with increasing real income is a more flexible work schedule, that, in other words, more workers would want intermittent employment and that as a result wage rates of workers on intermittent schedules would tend to fall relatively, a fall disguised to some extent by an increasing tendency for nominal wage rates to represent only a portion of total full-year earnings for full-year workers, intermittent workers being excluded from part of "fringe" benefits.

If, on the other hand, techniques for substituting intermittent workers for full-year workers become more sophisticated and there is no significant difference between the marginal product of a worker hired intermittently and one hired for a full-year period, then one would expect that wage differentials would remain relatively unchanged even if the desire for one type of work experience should increase relative to the other.

INVESTMENT IN HUMAN CAPITAL AND
PERIPHERAL WORK EXPERIENCE

Gary Becker, in his *Human Capital*, developed a concise but ingenious analytical scheme which enables him to frame several important hypotheses regarding the relationship between specific on-the-job training and general on-the-job training.

The analysis focuses on the question of the sharing of the costs of training and of the resulting yields between employer and employee.

Of critical importance in determining the sharing of costs and gains is the degree of specificity of the skills which are produced by the investment in training. In general, the more specific the skill, the more the employer bears the costs and reaps the gain.

In the course of his argument, Becker raises the following question:

Could not one equally well argue that workers pay all specific training costs by receiving appropriately lower wages initially and collect all returns by receiving wages equal to marginal product later? . . . Is it more plausible that firms rather than workers pay for and collect any return from training? [15]

Becker answers this question as follows:

If a firm had paid for the specific training of a worker who quit to take another job, its capital expenditures would be partly wasted, for no further return could be collected. Likewise, a worker fired after he had paid for specific training would be unable to collect any further return and would also suffer capital loss. The willingness of workers or firms to pay for specific training should, therefore, closely depend on the likelihood of labor turnover.[16]

He points out that "to bring in turnover . . . may seem like a *deus ex machina* since it is almost always ignored in traditional theory." The explanation of this slighting of labor turnover is the assumption of the traditional analysis of the competitive firm that wages equal marginal products at all times and that "marginal products are . . . the same in many firms" so that "no one suffers from turnover. It would not matter whether a firm's labor force always contained the same persons or a rapidly changing group." [17]

[15] Gary Becker, *Human Capital* (New York: National Bureau of Economic Research, 1964), p. 21.
[16] *Ibid.*   [17] *Ibid.*

As Becker sees it, the inclusion of the costs of training in the analysis changes the situation fundamentally:

Turnover becomes important when costs are imposed on workers or firms, which are precisely the effects of specific training. Suppose a firm paid all the specific training costs of a worker who quit after completing it. According to our earlier analysis, he would have been receiving the market wage and a new employee could be hired at the same wage. If the new employee were not given training, his marginal product would be less than that of the one who quit since presumably training raised the latter's productivity. Training could raise the new employee's productivity but would require additional expenditures by the firm. . . . In the same way an employee who pays for specific training would suffer a loss from being laid off because he could not find an equally good job elsewhere.[18]

Becker concludes that, since the quit rate is a function of the wage level, employers are therefore likely to "offer employees some of the return from training" but at the same time "to shift some of the training costs . . . to employees, thereby bringing supply more in line with demand." [19] It should be added that in the case of the costs of general training (where skills have general application to a number of firms) the worker himself must bear the cost of training and is free to recoup his investment either with the firm that trains him or with other firms. To the extent that any actual training consists of specific and general components, the costs and gains will be shared between employee and employer. Becker sums up the matter succinctly:

Since firms do not pay any of the completely general costs and only part of the completely specific costs, the fraction of the costs paid by the firms would be inversely related to the im-

---

[18] *Ibid.*, p. 22. Becker refers to Marshall's *Principles* (p. 26), where this situation engages Marshall's attention, and notes Marshall's conclusion that in such cases the wage rate is indeterminate, depending essentially upon the kinds of elements that enter into bilateral monopoly.

[19] Becker, *Human Capital*, p. 22.

portance of the general component, or positively related to the specificity of the training.[20]

There are several points that emerge when Becker's analysis of human capital is applied to the problem of the peripheral labor force. It would seem likely that in those industries where intermittent employment is an expected and chronic state of affairs for some employees there would be a tendency to a low rate of investment in the training of these workers by individual firms. However, this low rate of investment would be confined to the intermittent part of the firm's work force.

On the one hand, the expected rate of return for such training is a function of expected continuity of employment. On the other hand, where training is specific in character (and therefore the costs are ordinarily borne in part by the firm) the chances of intermittent employment leading to a change of employer are likely to be relatively high and are higher the longer the periods that intervene between spells of employment. Similarly, it would be difficult to shift some of the costs of training onto the worker in the form of reduced earnings during the period of training if the worker himself had no great confidence in his chances of employment continuity.

To the extent that intermittent employment of a worker takes the form of successive periods of employment experience with a single employer, this tendency to underinvestment in training of intermittent employees would be lessened. It would seem worth while to explore whether, in industries and occupations where intermittent employees display relatively strong degrees of attachment to a single employer over long periods of time, there is a significantly greater amount of on-the-job training than in those industries and occupations where by contrast there is a high degree of shifting from one firm to another on the part of employees.

Our hypothesis, then, is that one of the characteristics of

[20] *Ibid.*, p. 23.

intermittency of employment experience is a relative decrease in the amount of investment in specific on-the-job training. If this is correct, two or three consequences can be expected to flow from the situation that is created by this relative training deprivation of the individual worker. First of all, he is unable to share that part of the gains of specific training that accrues to employees. The second consequence is perhaps even more important. The very fact that the intermittent worker does not receive specific training is at the same time one of the reasons why his tie to the employer is weak and why he is more subject to intermittent employment. The employer has no capital sunk in the training of such a worker and therefore cannot lose any of this capital if the intermittent worker does not return to him after a spell of interrupted employment.

It seems probable that there is a further consequence, more indirect but more pervasive. Let us take a firm which has experienced considerable fluctuations of its total labor inputs over a number of years. According to our analysis, such a firm will be reluctant to make any investment in specific on-the-job training of those workers whose employment experience is expected to be intermittent. However, such a firm, it seems reasonable to suppose, must maintain a certain level of total skill in its labor force in order to carry out its operations. To the extent that the fluctuating component of its labor force is underskilled because it does not pay the firm to make any investment in the training of such workers, the firm may be forced to attempt to raise the skill level of that component of its labor force which has continuity of employment in order to compensate for the relatively unskilled character of the rest of its employees.

If this is the case, we can expect to find that there is a tendency for the labor force of such a firm to be strongly and permanently bifurcated. One branch will have a relatively high degree of continuity of employment and high wages since it has relatively a high degree of specific training. The remainder of the labor force of the firm will bear the entire burden of fluctuations of the firm's total inputs of labor over the course of time, but at the same time it will have to accept relatively low wages because the very fact of the intermittency of its employment experience has prevented any investment of capital in specific on-the-job training for this kind of employee. What has been said here about intermittent workers seems to be more or less applicable to workers whose employment experience is part time in character and is the more applicable to that large fraction of the peripheral labor force whose employment experience is at one and the same time intermittent and part time.

INCOME AND HOURS OF WORK

When they have turned their attention to the subject of labor, economists have usually been primarily interested in the determinants of wage rates. (Usually hourly wage rates are meant.) In other words, they have been more interested in labor as a cost than as a source of income for the individual worker. From the worker's point of view, of course, hours worked per week and weeks worked per year are just as much determinants of income as wages per hour.

The willingness of many economists, moreover, to permit standard hours of work to be set by government fiat stands in contrast with their opposition to wage rates set by the political process. It was often assumed that workers either worked the standard work week or did not work at all. The only means by which a general desire to work shorter hours could manifest itself was believed to be through trade union or governmental action. No individual firm could afford by itself to permit working hours to be shorter than the standard work week of the industry to which it belonged. The standard work week of a particular industry was, in this view, determined, in the absence of governmental intervention or trade union pressure, for the most part by technology on the one hand and the physical limitations of workers on the other. Moreover, an important implication of this view was that workers generally desired shorter hours than the standard work week at any moment of time. The political process which produced shorter hours necessarily took time and there was always some pressure of discontent with the standard hours before the political process could be set in motion.

As the theory of wage determination became more sophisticated, it was only to be expected that the theory would be applied to the problem of the determination of hours of work as well as to wages. The supply of any particular kind of labor is in the final analysis the resultant of the actions of individuals faced with a problem of allocating their limited amount of time between work and all other uses of time. The action system which eventuates in such an allocative decision seems to be neatly presented by means of an indifference map whose two axes represent respectively income and nonwork time (usually called leisure). The options available to an individual if the wage rate is constant no matter how many hours he chooses to work are summarized by a straight line originating at the point on the horizontal axis corresponding to zero hours of work, the slope of which is determined by the hourly wage rate. An individual's work income decision is rational when he acts so as to reach a point on the highest indifference curve available to him by moving along one of the wage-rate lines.

Some problems arise when we attempt to use this theoretical apparatus to analyze an individual's choice of how many hours he will work when he is free to vary his activity (i.e., when he faces a choice of different jobs at differing wage rates). One difficulty was noted by Marshall in the famous Chapter II of Book III of the *Principles*, "Wants in Relation to Activities."

The desire for the exercise and development of activities, spreading through every rank of society . . . leads not only to the pursuit of science, literature and art for their own sake, but to the rapidly increasing demand for the work of those who pursue them as professions. Leisure is used less and less as an opportunity for mere stagnation; and there is a growing desire for those amusements, such as athletic games and travelling, which develop activities rather than indulge any sensuous craving. . . . Speaking broadly therefore, although it is man's wants in the earliest stages of his development that give rise to his activities, yet afterwards each new step upwards is to be regarded as the development of new activities giving rise to new wants, rather than new wants giving rise to new activities. . . . It is not true, therefore, that "the Theory of Consumption is the scientific basis of economics." For much that is of chief interest in the science of wants, is borrowed from the science of efforts and activities. . . . But if either, more than the other, may claim to be the interpreter of the history of man, whether on the economic side or any other it is the science of activities and not that of wants.[21]

In terms of the problem of income-leisure choice, the point that Marshall makes here is that each possible activity produces its own unique set of evaluations of wants, including leisure. Marshall also notes that a change in the character and meaning of leisure itself has taken place.

Gary Becker calls attention to some neglected aspects of the economic significance of nonwork time in his article "A Theory of the Allocation of Time." [22] Becker, pointing out that time is required for consumption as well as for production, proposes a redefinition of the term "commodity." Traditionally a commodity has been something bought in a market. Becker suggests a new term, "market good," to represent the traditional "commodity." From the point of view of consumption, the market good is incomplete. It must still be combined

[21] Marshall, *Principles*, pp. 89–90.
[22] Gary Becker, "A Theory of the Allocation of Time," *Economic Journal*, September, 1965, pp. 493–517.

with a certain amount of time in order to be consumed. It is the market good plus the time required for its consumption which Becker calls a commodity. Becker's article presents "a theoretical analysis of choice that includes the cost of time on the same footing as the cost of market goods" and then goes on to discuss the implications of the theory with respect to work and leisure.

In the conventional analysis of an individual's choice of income and leisure, it is assumed that an individual allocates his time so that he can acquire a market basket of goods and services equal in value to the money income he has acquired by work *plus* a certain amount of leisure, the cost of which is represented by the money income he has forgone by not working all available hours. The market basket and the leisure both have utility in themselves. But in Becker's analysis nonworking time does not mean idle time. Rather it is a resource which must itself be efficiently allocated in combination with market goods to produce the commodities which ultimately produce utility. Leisure is not wanted for its own sake, rather it is desirable because of the activities it makes possible.

Economists have long asked whether the structure of the labor market and the existence of standard work weeks in various sectors of the economy make it possible for the individual worker to work close to an optimum number of hours per day. Can all the workers in a factory really want to work the same number of hours? According to Stigler, there are several reasons for suspecting that, contrary to what we might hastily conclude, the answer to this question may be "almost."

We should expect individuals to choose occupations and employers with some attention to their working characteristics. Moreover, the preferences of various individuals as to hours of work are not necessarily very different. Just as there are not enough consumers to support the production of any particular non-conventional style of automobile, there may be relatively few workers sufficiently different from the average of their occupation to prefer widely different working hours. The hours of work are not rigidly fixed in any occupation when one takes into account absenteeism, vacations, leave, etc.[23]

But the existence of various punitive measures—fines, delays in promotion and pay raises, even discharge—designed to prevent nonconformity to standard hours, as expressed by absenteeism, tardiness, or early departure, would seem to indicate that standard hours do mean that for many workers there is a fairly marked disequilibrium in the number of hours worked on any given day.

More serious questions in fact arise than the possibility that some workers are forced by standard hours to work more or less than they would like to. These problems cluster around what Marshall so aptly called the "centre of the chief difficulty of almost every economic problem . . . the element of Time." [24] Clearly the wants of an individual and the wage lines he can choose depend upon the past he has experienced and the future he contemplates. It is not just income on the day of choice that the worker must keep in mind. The choice of a particular income today implies an income stream which has a particular shape in the future. The rate of discount which an individual applies to future income streams—a rate which depends on such factors as life expectancy, uncertainties about the continuity of the income stream promised by different wage lines (each representing a different activity), uncertainties about the desirability of a lifetime of continuous work experience (particularly relevant in the case of women where shifting nonmarket productivities depend upon such contingencies as marriage, children, and widowhood)—can be expected to have some influence upon his present choice of hours

[23] George J. Stigler, *The Theory of Price* (Rev. ed.; New York: Macmillan, 1952), p. 200.

[24] Marshall, *Principles*, p. vii.

to work. We could, it is true, try to include all these elements in some concept of wages which represents the net advantages of different activities, but it is not at all clear what such an omnibus wage concept really would mean.

But it is not only the relation between present and future income that brings complexity into the neat analytical world of a single worker faced with the problem of choosing a particular combination of leisure and income. Past experience enters into the system only indirectly in the form of its influence upon the character of wants and upon the range of wage lines (activity lines) open to the individual. It is platitudinous to point out that the range of options open to an individual at any moment is determined by previous experience. For some people options become wider and richer as time passes. For others the range narrows until from their point of view freedom of choice seems almost nonexistent. Or, if options remain, there may be so little difference between their values that, rather than invest effort in making the choice, the individual prefers to let a flip of the coin decide for him.

Any adequate concept of human behavior recognizes that basic patterns of life tend to become habits. This is particularly true of work experience. At a very early age, a child, for example, is characterized by his "work habits," and it has long been recognized that for many individuals the abrupt breaking of lifetime patterns of work at retirement age produces profound and dangerous physical and psychic disorder and damage. In terms of the income-leisure choice facing an individual, this means that habituation tends to transform the factors that determine the choice over time and to narrow the range of choice. For at least some individuals who have worked an unvarying pattern of hours for many years, one of the requirements of any new job would be that it conform closely to this pattern. If such a worker, particularly an "older" worker, finds his full-time employment terminated, any intermittent or part-time employment may be profoundly disturbing to him. He finds it difficult to accept the fact that he can no longer command the wages of a full-time, full-year employee or that in the type of employment open to him there are constraints upon his work schedule. He finds it profoundly disquieting and humiliating to discover that he is no longer given the responsibilities that he used to have, that he is no longer a full-fledged member of a work group. He becomes a supernumerary. He discovers, if he never knew it before, the meaning of peripheral work.

SUMMARY

An explanation of what has happened to the "peripheral labor force" over the last half century or so in the United States must somehow manage to integrate an analysis which is centered on the process of commitment in all its social and anthropological complexity with another type of analysis which sees the "peripheral labor force" as a facet of the general problem that Gary Becker dealt with in his above-mentioned article. Becker's work would suggest that the development of part-time and intermittent work patterns in the United States can at least in part be explained by means of a generalized theory of consumer choice "that includes the cost of time on the same footing as the cost of market goods." [25]

As Becker puts it, the more general theory of consumer choice permits "a new approach to changes in hours of work and 'leisure.' " He points out that

a traditional "economic" interpretation of the secular decline in hours worked has stressed the growth in productivity of working time and the resulting income and substitution effects, with the former supposedly dominating. Ours stresses that the substitution effects of the growth in productivity of working and consumption time tended to offset each other and that hours worked declined

[25] Becker, "A Theory of the Allocation of Time," p. 494.

secularly primarily because time-intensive commodities have been luxuries. A contributing influence has been the secular decline in the relative prices of goods used in time-intensive commodities.[26]

Becker's analysis does not explicitly deal with the phenomena of part-time and intermittent work. But to the extent that such work patterns are indeed free economic choices, it should be possible to fit them into the theoretical framework expounded in his article. It may indeed be that part of the interest in the contrast between our recent experience of part-time and intermittent work and that of the turn of the century derives from the possibility that the two sets of phenomena are in large part of fundamentally different character and spring from differing causes.

The "peripheral labor force" of the turn of the century, perhaps an even larger share of the labor force than it is today, may have been in large part a phenomenon of acculturation in which the individual involved had a minimum of economic freedom (even though he may have felt that the work he performed was the kind that he wanted to perform and that the regular and disciplined work of the factory, the prototype of the industrial order in his mind, was abhorrent and unnatural).

The "new industrial" worker of those years was ruthlessly put through the mill. The social services that are taken for granted today and that might have supported him both psychologically and physically, giving him options, providing him with training and guidance, were almost totally absent. Industry did not undertake systematically to train him, to acculturate him. In fact, in many areas and industries the presence of a great mass of undigested labor, ready to take up work at a moment's notice, willing to accept termination of employment almost as readily, seems to have been positively desired. In an economy growing rapidly, with inevitable dislocations and

[26] *Ibid.*, p. 517.

imbalances, with technological change taking place more rapidly than any society had ever yet been forced to cope with, flexibility of production was peculiarly desirable. What better means of achieving the necessary flexibility than a labor force whose most unskilled members were so green and yet so tough that they could be expected to wander off somewhere else, living from hand to mouth, supporting each other somehow or other, when the tide of economic activity, either for a firm or an industry or perhaps for the entire economy, turned downward? They could always be expected to go somewhere else! After all, their first step into the industrial world had been, in so many cases, nothing but a flight from the intolerable past to that future "somewhere else," always to the West where hope seemed to lie.

Certainly, something like this process of acculturation may still be at work for some segments of society, but less and less accepted by the surrounding society, more and more apt to be interrupted or even stopped. Negroes being pushed out of the South seem from this vantage point simply another group in the process of being shaped by the mold of the industrial society and fated to go through a stage of being the contemporary "new industrial" worker.

But there seem to be major new elements in our society who are also participating in a world of work characterized by intermittency and part-time work patterns. For some of these, in particular for women and the elderly, it may be that work hours (and the schedules which permit them) are much more an expression of the kind of economic choice that Becker has in mind. These groups are not being molded or shaped or passing through any stage toward full commitment. Rather they are the harbingers of a new kind of labor force. Real income of the members will be sufficient for them to purchase, always with due regard to the cost of time both in consumption and in production, the kind of work schedules which fit their own tastes and income. For these individuals, being a member of the "peripheral labor force" does not mean wearing a badge of inferiority nor is it a confession that one is not yet a full-fledged member of society.

But even if this freedom of choice is now becoming possible to some, it remains true that our present "peripheral labor force" bears many of the scars and disabilities of the past and that there are important groups, particularly the nonwhite, who may be even more harshly subject to its disabilities and penalties than were the countless and diverse groups who made up this part of the labor force at the turn of the century. At that time their very numbers and diversity helped them to pass through the harsh years, allowed many of them to find a helping hand among those who had made the fearful trip somewhat earlier.

If industry in those days would not deliberately train and maintain its labor force, then the labor force itself had somehow to shift for itself and, as Ginzberg and Berman's *The American Worker* often recounts, the helping hand might be found at any time and at any place. One of the institutions which helped the immigrant to achieve stable employment, tolerable hours, status, and a sense of belonging to the industrial world was eventually to be the trade union. Seniority, pensions, grievance procedures, all were developments which permitted a sizable portion of the American labor force finally to attain full commitment.

If Clark Kerr is correct in his outline of the stages of commitment to work, social institutions that evolved in the process of the creation of this commitment possibly have an almost inevitable tendency to lead to overcommitment for some parts of the labor force.[27] But overcommitment for some is likely to

[27] See Clark Kerr, *Labor and Management in Industrial Society* (Garden City, N.Y.: Doubleday and Company, 1964), particularly Part IV, pp. 330–44.

be counterbalanced by undercommitment for others. The difference between the undercommitment of the 1900s and that of today may possibly be that the former was for many merely a stage in the transition to secure status, while today undercommitment may become for some groups of the population a permanent state. For these disadvantaged groups peripheral work experience may be, not a response to increasing income and options, but rather a result of institutions and economic factors at the center of the process of recruitment of full-time, full-year workers which inhibit their entry to secure status in the world of work.

⤙ CHAPTER V ⤚

THE STRUCTURE OF DEMAND FOR PERIPHERAL WORKERS

THE PURPOSE of this chapter is to fill in the details of the present structure of demand for peripheral workers in the United States. It attempts to provide a partial answer to these two related questions: Where are peripheral workers employed? What do they do? The occupations and industries in which part-time workers are found are so different from those using intermittent workers that it is desirable to keep the two groups separate.

THE DEMAND FOR PART-TIME WORKERS

INDUSTRIAL COMPOSITION

As might be expected, the employment of part-time workers is very heavily concentrated in a small number of industries. In 1965 two thirds of all part-time employment experience was accounted for by six industrial groups. By far the largest proportion was contributed by "retail trade," which alone accounted for more than one fifth of all part-time employment experience. Another sixth was accounted for by "private household service." On the other hand, the major manufacturing industries of the country, for all practical purposes, do not use part-time workers. Durable and nondurable goods manufacturing industries in 1965 together employed fewer part-time workers than were employed in education alone.

If industry groups are ranked by relative frequency of part-time employment experience (percentage of total part-time employment experience/percentage of total employment experience), a Lorenz-type curve can be constructed. The industries at the lower end of the scale which account collectively for 25 percent of total employment experience account for only 3 percent of total part-time employment experience. They include all the durable goods manufacturing industries with the exception of "lumber and wood products, excluding furniture"; three of the nondurable goods producing industries, "textile mill products," "chemicals and allied products," and "other nondurable goods"; and three of the transportation and public utilities industries, "railroads and railway express service," "communications," and "other public utilities." Finally two of the public administration industries are included, "federal public administration" and "state public administration."

In contrast, the industries at the upper end of the scale which account for 25 percent of total employment experience are service industries, agriculture (wage and salary workers and unpaid family workers), retail trade, and "nonagricultural unpaid family workers." Collectively they account for about 45 percent of part-time work experience.

To sum up, part-time work experience in recent years has been overwhelmingly concentrated in the following sectors of the economy: agriculture, services, and retail trade. It is practically nonexistent in the durable goods manufacturing sector, only slightly more in evidence in the nondurable goods manufacturing sector. Similarly it has been negligible in the railroad industry, the communication industries, and in other public utilities. Very few part-time workers are employed in federal and state administrations.

In other words, if an individual wishes to work part time, he or she can expect to find very few opportunities for such employment experience in the large-scale manufacturing industries, the utilities, and the state and federal bureaucracies. Of the almost 17½ million individuals whose work experience in 1965 was part time, less than 1.4 million were employed in these sectors.

Between 1959 and 1965 the number of individuals whose work experience was part time increased from 15.2 million to 17.5 million. The percentage share of most industries in these totals remained very stable. Two thirds of the increase in percentage shares over this period of time is accounted for by two industries, retail trade and education. Nonagricultural self-employment and the medical industry account for a good portion of the remainder. Most of the service industries, indeed, show some increase in percentage shares but their total increase is no greater than that of retail trade by itself (4.8 points).

Among those industries which manifested a decrease in percentage shares, two categories stand out. The most striking is "unpaid family workers." In 1959 one out of ten individuals with part-time work experience was an agricultural unpaid family worker. By 1965 this proportion had been reduced to only one out of twenty. The nonagricultural part-time unpaid family category also underwent a pronounced decrease in its percentage share, falling from 4.6 percent in 1959 to 2.2 percent in 1965.

Between 1959 and 1965, then, most industries maintained approximately an unaltered percentage share of total part-time work experience. Whatever shift in the industrial structure of part-time work that did take place was confined largely to agriculture as a whole and nonagricultural unpaid family workers on the one hand, accounting for three quarters of the total decline in percentage shares, and retail trade, education, nonagricultural self-employment, and the medical industry on the other hand, accounting for three quarters of the total increase in percentage shares.

The likelihood of a part-time worker being an agricultural worker decreased markedly. In 1959 one out of every five individuals with part-time work experience was found in the agricultural sector. By 1965 this proportion was reduced to one out of seven.

Many of the manufacturing industries have extremely small proportions of part-time workers in their work force. Less than 1 percent of all individuals with work experience in the automotive industry in 1965, for example, were part-time workers. In general those manufacturing industries characterized by the lowest percentage of part-time work experience are the mass production, durable goods industries where the typical firm has a high capital/labor ratio. In eight of the durable goods manufacturing industries less than 3 percent of the total number of individuals with work experience were part-time workers in 1965. Only in "lumber and wood products, excluding furniture" was as much as 10 percent of the total made up of part-time workers.

The percentage of those with work experience whose employment was part time was somewhat higher in the nondurable goods manufacturing industries than in the durable goods sector and in the case of the printing industry was conspicuously higher than in any other manufacturing industry. Slightly more than one out of four individuals with work experience in the printing industry was a part-time worker. The high proportion of nominal part-time workers in this industry, however, is in all probability simply a reflection of the fact that hours specified in union contracts have already fallen below the 35 hours that is the dividing line used by the monthly survey of the labor force in classifying workers as full time or part time. It is probable that the printing industry is largely composed of workers who are in fact heavily committed to the industry.

When we turn to those industries that have high proportions of part-time employment experience, the service industries are outstanding. With the exception of "finance, insurance, and real estate," part-time workers constituted 20 percent or more of all individuals with work experience in the service industries. One third of all individuals with work experience in retail trade and in "welfare and religious services" had part-time experience. The highest proportion of individuals with part-time work experience, however, is found in private household work, where seven out of ten individuals with work experience during 1965 worked part time.

Economic organizations that use large proportions of part-time workers are usually small-scale and service oriented. Part-time workers are also found in large proportions in several industries where working hours are unconventional. The entertainment industry and retail trade are the most conspicuous instances, but undoubtedly a good deal of the part-time work experience in other service industries, such as "business and repair services," "personal services, excluding private household," and "other professional services," reflects unconventional hours of work in these areas of the economy.

The part-time worker, then, is an extreme rarity in those industries whose typical firms are large-scale, bureaucratically organized, heavily capitalized organizations. This is particularly the case where the individual worker is a member of a complex in which his activity is part of a sequential production process. At the extreme, where the part-time worker is for all practical purposes not used at all, we find the automotive industry. Approximately one out of every one hundred and fifty male workers is on a part-time basis in this industry. The woman part-time worker is an even more extreme rarity. Only about one out of every ten workers in this industry is a woman and less than one out of every forty women is a part-time employee.

On the other hand, in the "service and finance" sector, which in 1965 employed altogether some 22.8 million workers, a million and a half more workers than the entire manufacturing sector, almost three out of ten workers were on a part-time basis. Moreover, it should be noted that this sector relies heavily upon women workers. Almost two out of three service workers are women. Only one out of five male service workers work part time, but one third of the women are part-time workers.

Within this broad sector, one industry, "finance, insurance, and real estate," is much less apt to use part-time employees. Since this industry includes banks and insurance companies that are large-scale bureaucracies, it is worth while separating them along with two other service industries which are characterized, at least in part, by large-scale bureaucratic organization, the "educational" industry and the "medical and other health services industry," from the other service industries. The remainder of the service industries are by and large made up of small firms or of workers who are employed as individuals to render direct services largely to consumers. Some ten million individuals are in these service industries, almost two out of three of whom are women. More than 40 percent of the workers in the service industries are part-time workers. One quarter of the males work part time, one half of all the women.

Among those industries where the part-time percentage share increased between 1959 and 1965, retail trade stands out. One quarter of all individuals in retail trade in 1959 had part-time work experience. By 1965 the proportion had risen to one third. This enormous increase is accounted for in part by the increase in the proportion of total part-time employment experience in the retail trade industry. But it is also a reflection that work experience in retail trade grew relatively much faster than work experience as a whole. The segment of the population with work experience during the year grew 10 percent between 1959 and 1965. Work experience in retail trade, however, increased by 15 percent. As a result, the number of individuals who had part-time work experience in retail trade grew by one and a quarter million.

Indeed, if we combine the increase in the number of individuals with part-time work experience in retail trade with the increase in the service industries, we find that there was an increase of almost three million persons in these two areas alone between 1959 and 1965. This exceeds the total increase in all kinds of work experience, full time, intermittent, and part time, in the entire manufacturing sector over this same period of time by more than half a million.

It is important, however, to note that in the service sector as a whole there was only a slight increase in the percentage share of total part-time work experience. The increase in the number of individuals in the service sector whose work experience was part time is accounted for largely by the very rapid growth rate of work experience as a whole in this sector. The number of individuals with work experience in the service sector grew by 27.5 percent between 1959 and 1965.

In several of the service industries, however, a marked increase in the percentage share of total part-time work experience did take place. These include "entertainment," "private household work," "education," and "business and repair services."

THE OCCUPATIONAL COMPOSITION OF
PART-TIME WORK EXPERIENCE

The industrial composition of part-time employment experience helps to throw light on the demand for part-time workers. It tells us in what sectors of the economy they are most apt to be found and what kinds of industries use them relatively most heavily. But by itself the industrial composition of part-time work experience does not tell us what the part-time worker does. A more complete sense of the character of the demand for such workers is provided by adding what is known about their occupational characteristics to what is known about their industrial location in the economy. To some extent, of course, the occupational composition of part-time employment experience is foreshadowed by what we have said about its industrial composition, since occupations and industries are highly correlated. Nevertheless, the broad occupational distribution of part-time employment experience is an important dimension of peripheral work experience. In several occupations the part-time worker is almost unknown. In others he is relatively common. For example, more than a third of the waiters, cooks, and bartenders of the country have primarily part-time work experience, as do almost one half of the retail sales workers. On the other hand, in the category "foremen, not elsewhere classified," which includes the vast majority of shop supervisory personnel in the manufacturing industry—slightly more than one and a half million individuals in 1965—only 0.7 percent have primarily part-time work experience. In 1965, a year of relatively high employment levels, the skilled craftsmen in the manufacturing industry belonged to those occupations in which part-time employment experience was least common.

Several additional details bear notice. First of all, the general category of "operatives" displays marked variation. One out of thirty operatives in the durable goods manufacturing sector had primarily part-time work experience in 1965. One out of fifteen operatives in the nondurable goods manufacturing sector had this kind of employment experience. But almost one out of four operatives in the category "other industries" had primarily part-time work experience. Lest it be thought that this last group is a relatively small category, it should be pointed out that it constitutes almost one third of all operatives, almost as many as in either durable or nondurable goods manufacturing. Laborers in the manufacturing sector are characterized by a much higher proportion of part-time work experience than workers in other occupations found in this sector. Almost one out of six laborers in manufacturing had primarily part-time work experience in 1965.

Between 1959 and 1965 two blue-collar occupations, construction laborers and nondurable operatives, showed marked decreases in the amount of total part-time work experience. On the other hand, in the case of a number of occupations, both blue-collar and white-collar, the percentage of part-time work experience went up considerably. It is interesting to contrast developments in the case of construction laborers with developments in the case of other types of laborer occupations, the laborer in manufacturing and the laborer in "other industries." Among other occupations in which part-time work experience accounted for significantly higher percentages of total work experience were a number of service occupations, reflecting the general shift to part-time work experience that has already been noted in the service industries. The most pronounced shift to part-time work experience took place among retail sales workers. In 1959, 38.5 percent of such workers had primarily part-time work experience. In 1965 almost one out of every two individuals whose occupation was retail sales was a part-time worker.

There is great variation among occupations in the proportion of total part-time work experience. However, one fact may at first seem somewhat surprising. There is no tendency for blue-collar occupations to cluster together among those occupations where the percentage of part-time work experience is high. It is only when a blue-collar worker is attached to

an industry where the typical firm is small-scale, either agricultural or service in character, that we find extremely high
rates of part-time work experience. The three occupations
which have the lowest rates of part-time work experience are
all blue-collar, but they are also occupations which are found
in the heavily capitalized, large-scale, durable goods producing
industries of the economy. Part-time work experience, therefore, is a pronounced characteristic of some blue-collar
occupations while almost unknown in others. In general, those
blue-collar occupations which have low rates of part-time
work experience are also occupations of high skill and status.
However, it is worth remarking again that operatives in both
durable and nondurable goods producing industries have relatively low rates of part-time experience.

Another question related to occupations involves the percentage share which individual occupations contribute to the
total number of individuals whose work experience is primarily part time during the course of the year. Four occupations account for almost one half of the total. One of seven
individuals with primarily part-time work experience in 1965
was classified by occupation as a "private household" worker.
But the likelihood that a person whose work experience in that
year was part time was occupationally classified as an "other
clerical" worker was almost as great. One out of every ten
individuals whose work experience was part time was a "retail
sales" worker. And almost as many individuals with part-time
work experience were in the occupational category "other
service workers."

If we examine the share of part-time work experience contributed by the various occupations, we find a remarkable
difference between those occupations whose contribution is
relatively large and those whose contribution is relatively low.
In 1965 the following occupations accounted for less than one
out of thirty individuals whose work experience was primarily

part time: foremen, not elsewhere classified; metal craftsmen; operatives in durable goods manufacturing; mechanics and repairmen; and "other craftsmen." More than one out of every three individuals with part-time work experience was a member of one of these six blue-collar occupations: private household workers, unpaid farm workers, retail sales workers, paid farm workers, laborers in other industries, waiters, cooks, and bartenders.

In summary, then, part-time work experience is highly concentrated within a narrow group of industries and occupations. In a number of industries and occupations the part-time worker is scarcely known. These industries are characterized by one or more of the following attributes: large-scale plants, bureaucratic organization, heavy capital investment per worker, sequential work processes. The individuals whose work experience is primarily part time are found predominantly in three areas of the economy: agriculture, retail sales, and some of the service sector.

The occupations where the part-time worker is apt to be found are those in which there is in general a relatively low level of skill. However, there is no marked tendency for the incidence of part-time work experience to be heavier in blue-collar occupations than in white-collar occupations. Moreover, several of the blue-collar occupations are among the lowest in rates of part-time work experience. Within broad occupational groups such as all operatives or all laborers, there is a marked difference in rates of part-time work experience when the occupation is broken down into subgroups by sector of activity.

THE DEMAND FOR
INTERMITTENT WORKERS

In 1965 the total population of peripheral workers as we have defined the term consisted of 37.8 million people, 17.5 million

of whom were individuals whose work experience during the
year was primarily part time in character. The remainder of
the peripheral population, full-time workers who worked less
than 50 weeks during the year, consisted of slightly more than
9 million individuals whose work experience was 1 to 26 weeks
in length and slightly more than 11 million whose work experience was 27 to 49 weeks in length. The first group is made up
of those workers whose work experience lasted no more than
half the year. As in the case of part-time workers, two questions are of interest. First of all, what industries and occupations accounted for relatively large percentage shares of this
kind of employment experience? (In what follows the worker
who worked full time a half year or less will be called an
intermittent worker, following the usage in Chapter 4,
"Trends in the Part-Time Labor Force," in Gertrude Bancroft's *The American Labor Force.*) Second, what industries
and occupations have high proportions of intermittent
workers?

INDUSTRIAL COMPOSITION

One industry alone, "retail sales," accounted for one sixth of
all intermittent employment in 1965. About one out of every
eleven intermittent workers was employed in agriculture.
"Paid agricultural laborers and foremen" accounted for one
out of every fifteen intermittent workers, about the same proportion as the construction industry was responsible for. The
medical and educational industries each accounted for about
one out of every eighteen intermittent workers.

Although these five industry groups accounted for more
than 40 percent of all intermittent employment in 1965, intermittent work experience was much more widely dispersed
among the major industrial groups than was the case of part-
time work experience. The reader may recall that those industries accounting for 25 percent of all work experience which
at the same time made relatively small use of part-time

workers employed only 3 percent of such individuals. At the other extreme, industries which accounted for 25 percent of all individuals with work experience but made extensive use of part-time workers employed 55 percent of such workers. In vivid contrast, those industries with relatively low rates of intermittent work experience, accounting for 25 percent of all individuals with work experience, employed 13 percent of all intermittent workers. Moreover, the manufacturing industries are not included among those industries with low rates of intermittent work experience. This is again in contrast to the case of part-time work experience where the manufacturing industries, both durable and nondurable, are in general characterized by rates of part-time work experience that are far lower than the service industries.

Between 1959 and 1965 most industries maintained about the same share of all intermittent workers. The share accounted for by retail sales, however, fell by 2.3 percentage points. Agricultural wage and salary workers, 6.8 percent of all intermittent workers in 1965, made up 8.4 percent of the total in 1959. Private household workers accounted for almost 5 percent of all intermittent workers in 1959; by 1965 their percentage share had fallen to 3.7 percent. A good part of the increase in percentage shares was attributable to two industries. Both education and the medical industry accounted for a much higher proportion of all intermittent workers in 1965 than they had in 1959, education increasing from 3.7 percent to 5.7 percent of the total, medical and other health industries rising from 3.9 percent to 5.9 percent.

Among persons with work experience, the proportion with intermittent work experience scarcely altered between 1959 and 1965, being slightly more than 10 percent in both years. But there were a number of industries in which a marked change took place in the percentage of work experience accounted for by intermittent workers. The largest decrease occurred in the category "other durable goods manufacturing." In 1959 this category was among those that had the highest proportion of intermittent work experience. By 1965 it was among the lowest third of all industry groups in percentage of intermittent workers. The post office was another area in which there was a marked decrease in the proportion of intermittent work experience. By 1965 the post office had the smallest proportion of intermittent workers among all industry groups which employed workers. The three other categories which ranked with the post office were two "self-employed" categories and the category of "unpaid nonagricultural family workers."

However, by 1965 a pattern, not evident in 1959, is apparent in the ranking of industries by proportion of intermittent work experience. Among the fourteen industry groups in which the percentage of intermittent work experience was 8.0 percent or less, all are found in three sectors of the economy: (1) public administration, (2) transportation and other public utilities, and (3) "durable goods manufacturing" with the exception of the two categories of the "self-employed" and the category of "unpaid nonagricultural family workers." All three of these latter categories tend to have large proportions of part-time workers.

In 1965, then, the large-scale, heavily capitalized, and/or bureaucratic organizations found in durable goods manufacturing, transportation, public utilities, and public administration had unusually low rates of both intermittent and part-time work experience. At the other extreme, among those industry groups where intermittent work experience percentages were high in 1965 are industry groups in which part-time work experience rates were also high. They include a number of service industries and in particular retail sales. Among the manufacturing industries with high rates of intermittent work experience the "apparel" and the "food and kindred products" industries ranked highest. Finally we should note that there was a marked decrease in the percentage share of intermittent work experience in the automobile industry.

OCCUPATIONAL DISTRIBUTION OF
INTERMITTENT WORK EXPERIENCE

Stenographers and other clerical workers together account for one fifth of the total number of individuals whose work experience was intermittent in 1965. Operatives account for almost another fifth. Slightly less than one fifth is made up of service workers. Almost one out of every ten intermittent workers is a laborer.

At the other extreme, those occupations which contribute relatively small amounts of intermittent work experience to the economy are the managerial and skilled crafts groups. Only one of twenty intermittent workers in 1965 was in the broad occupational category "craftsmen, firemen, and kindred workers," although this occupation group contained 11 percent of all individuals with work experience. The "managerial, officials and proprietors, except farm" category accounted for almost 9 percent of all work experience, but only 2.6 percent of all intermittent work experience.

Between 1959 and 1965 four occupational groups displayed marked decreases in the percentage share of total intermittent work they had accounted for in 1959. Three of these were blue-collar occupations: "operatives in industries other than durable or nondurable goods manufacturing," "construction laborers," and "paid farm laborers and foremen." "Retail sales workers" constituted the fourth group. Among those occupations which accounted for an increased proportion of intermittent work, two were blue-collar—"laborers in manufacturing" and "operatives in nondurable goods manufacturing"—three were white-collar occupations—"other professional, technical, and kindred workers," "stenographers, typists, and secretaries," and "other clerical and kindred workers"—and one was the occupational group entitled "other service workers."

The following general statement about the occupational distribution of intermittent work experience seems justified. Although some blue-collar occupations have relatively high rates of intermittent work experience, they tend to be occupations associated with low levels of skill and income. Included in the group, however, are "clerical and kindred workers," a broad occupational category which because of its size (it accounted for more than 15 percent of all work experience in 1965) employed a large fraction of the total of intermittent workers. White-collar occupations as a whole accounted for a slightly larger proportion of total intermittent work experience in 1965 than they did in 1959 (37.5 percent as against 36.2 percent).

In half the major occupation groups at least one out of every ten individuals with work experience was an intermittent worker. Almost one out of four paid farm workers was an intermittent worker. More than one out of every five laborers in manufacturing industries worked intermittently, a much higher proportion than in the other two laborer occupational categories. In all but one of the "craftsmen" occupational categories, on the other hand, less than one out of every twenty workers was employed full time a half year or less. The exception, of course, was the "construction craftsmen" group.

CHAPTER VI

THE SOURCES OF SUPPLY
OF PERIPHERAL WORKERS

IN CHAPTER V two questions were asked: Where and by whom is the peripheral worker employed? What does he do in this employment? In this chapter the questions are: Who is the peripheral worker? What are some of his important characteristics? We have already had occasion to notice that to a very pronounced degree the supply of part-time and/or intermittent workers in the United States is drawn from quite specific demographic subgroups of the population.

This amounts to saying that the white adult male age groups furnish relatively few peripheral workers in our society. In 1965, for example, white males aged 25 to 44 accounted for almost 22 percent of all individuals with work experience during the year, but they accounted for only slightly more than 2 percent of all part-time work experience and less than 6 percent of all those whose full-time work experience lasted a half year or less.

The demographic groups whose peripheral work experience we will examine in this chapter are the following:

a) Women, with particular emphasis upon women in the central age groups, 25 to 54 years old.

b) Youth, including under that term all individuals under 25 years of age who have work experience.

c) Older workers, in particular those 55 years of age or older.

d) Nonwhites of all age groups.

There is an unavoidable overlap between these demographic groups. We will, for example, want to examine the experience of all nonwhites, regardless of age or sex, in one section.

In 1965 some 86 million people had work experience during the course of the year. This population can be subdivided into the following groups:

a) Women, aged 25 to 54, constituting slightly more than one fifth of all individuals with work experience, but making up 30 percent of all individuals with primarily part-time work experience and one quarter of all workers who worked full time a half year or less.

b) Individuals between the ages of 14 and 24, accounting for slightly less than one quarter of all individuals with work experience of any kind in 1965. This age group, however, accounted for almost one half of all individuals whose work experience was primarily part time in character and for more than one half of all individuals whose work experience was full time for a half year or less.

c) Individuals at least 55 years old, one sixth of all those with work experience, but accounting for almost one fifth of all part-time work experience. However, only about one out of every ten persons whose full-time work experience lasted no longer than half a year was 55 years or older.

d) Males, aged 25 to 54, making up 36 percent of all individuals with work experience during 1965, but accounting for less than 5 percent of all individuals with primarily part-time work experience and only 10 percent of those who worked full time a half year or less.

Table 6.1 presents a summary account of the relative contributions to part-time and intermittent work experience in

1965 of these four demographic groups, along with the contribution of two other groups, white males aged 25 to 44 and nonwhite males of the same age group. A simple index of each group's relative contribution to part-time and intermittent work experience has been calculated by dividing each group's share of total work experience of all kinds into its share of (*a*) part-time work experience and (*b*) intermittent work experience.

Table 6.1. *Relative Contribution of Selected Demographic Groups to Part-Time and Intermittent Work Experience, 1965*

Demographic Group	(1) Percent of Total Work Experience	(2) Percent of Intermittent Work Experience	(3) Index of Intermittency 2 ÷ 1	(4) Percent of Part-Time Work Experience	(5) Index of Part-Time Incidence 4 ÷ 1
Youth, aged 14 to 24	23.9	52.2	2.18	46.6	1.95
Older workers, aged 55 or older	17.9	11.3	0.63	19.1	1.07
Females, aged 25 to 54	22.0	25.6	1.16	29.6	1.35
Males, aged 25 to 54	36.2	10.7	0.30	4.6	0.13
	100.0	100.0		100.0	
White males, aged 25 to 44	22.0	5.6	0.25	2.4	0.11
Nonwhite males, aged 25 to 44	2.5	1.4	0.56	0.7	0.28

Table 6.1 serves to illustrate that it is women and the young who constitute much the larger part of the total supply of individuals with part-time and/or intermittent work experience, the two groups together accounting for almost four fifths in the case of part-time work experience and over three

quarters in the case of intermittent work experience. As might be expected, these two groups also score much higher on a rough scale designed to show the relative incidence of part-time and intermittent work experience in each of the six demographic groups.

White males, aged 25 to 44, are relatively uninvolved in part-time work experience; they are somewhat more affected by intermittency but far less than other groups. What is true of this group is more or less true of all males aged 25 to 54, but it should be noted that the experience of nonwhite males is markedly more peripheral. At the same time, nonwhite males show relatively less intermittency than do older workers and considerably less incidence of part-time work experience.

WOMEN AND THE
PERIPHERAL LABOR FORCE

Among the groups who at the present time compose the peripheral labor force women constitute by far the largest number. Slightly over 20.5 million women were in the peripheral labor force in 1965. Almost one fourth of all individuals who had work experience in 1965 were women who either worked less than a full year at full-time jobs or worked various periods of time at part-time jobs. Of women with work experience, more than six out of ten were peripheral workers. For comparison, nonwhites who were in the peripheral labor force in 1965 numbered slightly more than 5 million; youth (including everybody in the age groups 14 to 24), slightly more than fifteen million; and older workers (everybody aged 55 or over), slightly more than 6.5 million. The boundaries of these categories of course overlap. If we consider only those women in the central age group, 25 to 54, we find that they accounted for approximately 19 million of all females with work experience (33.1 million), and of this 19 million slightly more than

8.4 million (or 45 percent) worked full-time, full-year schedules. Even among the central age group of women, therefore, a very substantial number (some 10.5 million workers) are members of the peripheral labor force.

A breakdown of this central age group into ten-year age brackets, 25–34, 35–44, and 45–54, reveals, however, quite marked increases in the proportion of full-time, full-year workers as we move from the younger to the older age brackets. In the lowest age group only 38 percent worked full time the year round, while almost one half of women between 45 and 54 years of age worked full-time, full-year schedules. In contrast, almost 80 percent of men between the ages of 25 and 34 worked full time the full year and over 80 percent of the two next older age groups was accounted for by full-time, full-year workers. Women workers between 55 and 59 years of age tended to be even more concentrated in the category of full-year work experience. Moreover, about five out of six women in this age category who worked full-year schedules also worked full time.

It is of course impossible to come to any conclusion about the attachment of women to work, particularly women who are in the process of reentering the labor market after the formation of their families, until we take into consideration the extent to which the total population of women is involved, even for a short period of time, in work experience during the year. For all groups, 25–34, 35–44, and 45–54, more than half of the total population of women had some work experience during the course of 1965, the proportion reaching a peak of 58 percent for the age group 45–54.

The pronounced difference between the attachment of men and women to the world of work is illustrated by a comparison by age groups of the proportion of women who work full time all the year with the proportion of men who have similar work experience.

At the other extreme of attachment, those who work part time for 13 weeks or less, we find that for the male age groups the percentage of those who have such highly peripheral work experience is negligible (less than 0.5 percent), while for women the proportion is only about 4 percent for the age groups 25–34 and 35–44, falling to about 3 percent for women aged 45–54.

Age Group	Percent of Total Population Who Work Full-Year, Full-Time Schedules	
	Male	Female
25–34	77	19
35–44	82	25
45–54	79	28

Even though the mature woman's attachment to full-time, full-year work activity is very much below that of her male counterpart, it is an important social fact that almost one quarter of all women between the ages of 45 and 54 were full-time workers the year round. And it should be noted that, as we go from the younger age groups to age group 55–59, the proportion of women who worked such schedules scarcely changed, while for men the proportion continued its gradual decline from the high point of more than eight out of ten on year-round schedules for the age group 35–44. For men aged 55–59, the proportion of year-round workers fell to only slightly more than seven out of ten.

Even though a very large number of women work full-time, full-year schedules (if all age groups are included, some thirteen million women do so), in 1965 the only age group in which as much as 50 percent of the women had such work experience was the age group 55–59. For all women with work experience, 18 years old or over, about four out of ten were full-time, full-year workers. The proportion of men 18 years old and over with work experience who worked full time was approximately seven out of ten. In other words, for those women who have any commitment at all to work (i.e., who have any work experience during the course of a year), the discrepancy between the proportion of them who have a full commitment and the proportion of men who are fully committed is not so great as might be imagined. In 1966 some forty-eight million Americans were full-time, full-year workers and of this total slightly more than one quarter were women.

Though women, therefore, contribute a substantial portion of the fully committed workers in the American economy today, they at the same time account for a good deal more than one half of the peripheral labor force. Some 20.7 million women workers fell into this category in 1965 compared with only about 17.1 million men. Such a vast number of individual women obviously includes the most heterogeneous sets of work experience. Some light is thrown upon this heterogeneity when we examine their work experience from two different points of view. First of all, there is the question of how this work experience is distributed among different sectors of the economy and among different industries. Second, it is important to locate those occupations in which women's work experience is characteristically peripheral.

INDUSTRIAL AND SECTORAL COMPOSITION
OF PERIPHERAL WORK BY WOMEN

One of the most striking aspects of peripheral work activity of women is the difference between their work experience in manufacturing on the one hand and in all other industries on the other. Part-time employment, as distinct from part-year but full-time employment while working, accounts for only a very small proportion of the work experience of women in almost all manufacturing industries, durable and nondurable. In all durable goods industries taken together, for example, the proportion of the female work force that works part time is only 4.8 percent.

In nondurable industries, taken as a whole, approximately one woman in ten is employed in a part-time status. But this is largely because two of the nondurable industries, printing and food and kindred products, tend to employ a much larger proportion of part-time women than the rest of the nondurable industries. In printing, publishing, and allied industries, almost one woman in four is employed on a part-time basis; and in the very large food and kindred products industry about one woman in eight is a part-time worker. For the remainder of the nondurable goods industries the proportions of part-time women employees are approximately as low as they are in the durable goods industries.

Part-time employment of women, therefore, is found largely in either the trade sector or the service sector. These two sectors together were responsible for slightly more than 70 percent of all wage and salary employment of women in 1965 (approximately 21 million women). Of the approximately 8.4 million women who were wage and salary workers and who worked part time in 1965, 7.5 million were employed either in trade or in one of the service industries.

In the trade sector, nine out of ten women work in the retail category, and it is this area of the trade sector which is particularly characterized by peripheral work by women. Four out of ten women in retail trade are part-time workers; only three out of ten have full-time jobs throughout the year and almost two out of ten, although employed full time, work only half a year or less.

Part-time work experience is extremely varied in its incidence among the major subdivisions of the service sector. For example, the more than three million women who do service work in private households are predominantly part-time workers. More than two thirds of them work part time; only one out of seven is a full-time worker for the entire year. Of those who work full time, one third work less than half a year. On the other hand, women who work in finance, insurance, and real estate are apt to be full-time, full-year workers, almost six out of ten falling into this category. Only one out of seven women workers in this large subdivision (1.8 million) is a part-time employee.

In the two other subdivisions of the service sector which, along with private household work, are the major fields for women workers—medical and other health services with more than 2½ million workers and educational services with 3.4 million—part-time work accounts for only about two out of ten workers. Just under one half of all women who work in the medical area are full-time, full-year employees. In education only one out of three women is a full-year worker on a full-time basis. However, it is probable that the practice which is prevalent in some areas of not considering teachers to be employed during summer vacations results in many women teachers who are actually full-time members of schools and employed for both semesters being classified among those who work from 27 to 49 weeks. Almost one third of all women who work in the educational area are found in this category. It can reasonably be concluded that education is an area where there is a high concentration of women workers who according to the conventions of society would be considered full-time, full-year workers. The fact, however, that two out of ten women who work in the educational sector are now part-time employees indicates that it is possible that there is a potential supply of women who might be able to work part-time schedules in education if school systems were to increase the number of opportunities available for women to work part time.

Not surprisingly, the proportion of women workers in the public administration sector who work full-time, full-year schedules is very high. In both federal and state public administration employment some seven out of ten women workers are full-time employees the year round. Postal and local public administration female employees are less apt to work such schedules, but even in these cases approximately one out of two women works full time the full year. The proportion of women workers who work part-time schedules is very low, 6 percent for federal employees and 9 percent for state employees. However, in the postal service and in local public administration almost one out of three women works part time.

Finally we should note that the "self-employed" and the "unpaid family worker" categories, together accounting for only about one tenth of all women workers, are characterized by a considerable amount of part-time employment. Some six out of ten female unpaid family workers worked part time in 1965 and more than four out of ten self employed women reported themselves as part-time workers.

Summing up the character of part-time employment by sex, one is struck by the fact that in a number of industries, largely in the manufacturing sector, part-time employment of women is very much a rarity, in many cases accounting for less than 5 percent of the total female work force in an industry. On the other hand, there are several sectors and subsectors where part-time employment is more characteristic of the female labor force than full-time, full-year employment, in several cases approaching 50 percent of the female labor force and in the case of agriculture, in which 1.7 million women had work experience, accounting for two thirds of the female labor force.

An important dimension of part-time employment is the extent to which part-time employment of women is associated with part-year employment. The work experience data for 1965 reveal a very clear association of part-time employment with much less than full-year employment in the great majority of industries. For all industries combined, about three out of ten part-time women workers are employed for the entire year. For many industries the percentage of women part-time workers who work less than 27 weeks is substantially above 50 percent.

PART-TIME AND PART-YEAR EMPLOYMENT OF WOMEN BY OCCUPATION

An examination of employment experience of women by occupation reveals several interesting patterns which contrast strongly with the experience of male workers. Perhaps the most striking is the marked difference in the incidence of part-time employment among women professional, technical, and kindred workers compared with their male counterparts. Much of the difference here is probably due not merely to women having different employment experience in exactly identical occupations but also, and perhaps largely, to women being concentrated in certain professions, such as nursing, where part-time schedules are traditionally common. Whatever the explanation, it is still remarkable that while only one out of fifteen male professional workers is a part-time worker, more than one out of five women professionals are on part time. Women professional workers in the medical and health fields (numbering more than one million) have radically differing employment experience from men in the same fields. Four fifths of the men in these fields are full-time, full-year workers. Less than one half of all women in these fields work full time the entire year and about one quarter are part-time workers. A somewhat similar pattern emerges in the very large category of women teachers, except college (more than 1.5 million). While part-time employment is almost unknown among men teachers, one out of seven women teachers is a part-time teacher. While about six out of ten male teachers are full-time, full-year employees, only three out of ten women teachers have similar schedules.

Both men and women teachers frequently work between 27 and 49 weeks. However, it is more common for men to find full-year employment with their school systems than for women. Summer programs may tend to favor men teachers. On the other hand, women teachers, even when summer employment is offered, may be less inclined, or under less pressure, to accept such employment. It would seem, therefore, that there is a pool of women teachers available for summer educational programs if such programs were to be developed in a systematic and aggressive manner. It is understandable that women teachers may need several years of adjustment to break the pattern of no summer employment for a larger proportion of women teachers than of men.

Turning to other occupations of high status, we find that the tendency of women to occupy a part-time status is even more pronounced than it is in the medical and educational professions. Almost three out of ten of the 1.4 million women who are in the "other professional" category are part-time employees. This situation contrasts radically with that of men professional workers in this category, only one out of twenty of whom works part time. On the other hand, only four out of ten such professional women are full-time employees the year round. Again, men professional workers in this broad category are much more apt to work full time the entire year, some 80 percent having this employment experience.

Other occupations carrying high status are in the "managerial, officials and proprietors, except farm" category. Here again there is a marked difference between the work experience of women and men in so far as part-time employment is concerned. A negligible proportion of men are part-time workers (less than 4 percent) while one out of every six women in this occupational group is a part-time worker. On the other hand, we find that there is a rather high proportion of women in these occupations who work full time the year round. This is particularly true of salaried women managers and officials, some seven out of ten of whom work full time for the entire year. Men salaried managers and officials, it might be noted, are overwhelmingly full-time workers the year round, nine out of ten having this status. Both men and women in this occupational category, therefore, are conspicuously more apt to be full-time employees the year round than in the case of any other occupational group except for the category of "foremen, not elsewhere classified" where the proportion of full-time, full-year workers follows a very similar pattern.

With respect to the very large occupational group "operatives and kindred workers," a markedly different pattern of attachment to the world of work compared with that of the professional and managerial woman is clearly evident from the work experience data of 1965. While a large proportion of women professional workers, over 20 percent, and a somewhat small proportion of women managers and officials work part-time schedules, we find that, in the two large occupational categories of women operatives in durable goods and nondurable goods manufacturing, part-time employment is very much less common. Indeed, for the more than one million women who are operatives in durable goods industries, part-time employment is an extremely rare occurrence, only one out of some twenty-five women operatives having such employment experience in this sector of the economy during 1965. Even in the nondurable goods manufacturing sector only about one woman in twelve was a part-time worker.

At the same time, however, the female operative in these sectors is not apt to be a full-time, full-year worker. While some seven out of ten male operatives in the durable and nondurable manufacturing sectors work full time the year round, only 50 percent of women operatives in the durable goods manufacturing sector are full-time workers the year round and the percentage falls to 45 for the nondurable sector. The characteristic, therefore, which distinguishes women operatives from men operatives is the extent to which women, as compared to men, work full-time schedules for less than 50 weeks during the year. Slightly less than one quarter of women operatives work between 27 and 49 weeks on full-time schedules and one out of five works 26 weeks or less. In contrast, only one male operative out of eleven in the durable and non-durable goods manufacturing sectors works full time less than 27 weeks. In other words, the peripherality of women operatives tends to take more the form of a short work year rather than part-time employment.

Of the remaining large occupational groups in which women are found, only the "clerical and kindred workers" category has a large proportion of women who are employed full time the year round. Almost six out of ten stenographers, typists, and secretaries, for example, are full time, full year workers; slightly less than one out of seven is a part-time employee.

Finally there are several occupations which are marked by a very pronounced degree of peripherality, taking the form either of part-time employment or of very short work years. Some seven and a half million women, or almost one quarter of all women workers during 1965, were in the following occupations: sales workers (2.7 million), private household workers (3.3 million), and farm laborers (1.5 million). It is worth noting that these are occupations which in general are not clearly defined, are of relatively low skill levels, and tend to be synonymous with industrial categories. In each of these occupations part-time work is the predominant form of work experience for women, ranging from slightly over 50 percent for sales workers and paid farm workers to nearly 70 percent for private household service workers and almost 80 percent for unpaid family farm workers. Full-time work is of course the exception for these occupations. Only one quarter of the almost 2.4 million women retail sales workers have full-time, full-year jobs. The proportions of private household service workers and women farm workers who have full-time, full-year jobs is negligible, one out of seven in the case of the former and less than one out of ten for the latter.

One other occupational category in which women play an important role, "service workers other than private household," displays very strong peripheral characteristics, but in this case the pattern is somewhat different. Although only three of ten women in this occupation have full-time employment the year round, women in this occupational category are slightly more apt to have full-time employment for part of the year than they are to have part-time jobs. Approximately one third work part-time schedules.

The wide diversity of the work experience of women, both by industry and by occupation, is, as indicated previously, a major social fact. Of the thirty-four million women of all ages who had work experience in 1965, approximately one third worked at part-time jobs (many of which were, it should be noted, only part-year jobs also); a little less than a third worked full time for less than a full year, this group being about evenly divided between those who worked from 1 to 26 weeks and those who worked between 27 and 49 weeks; and, finally, slightly more than one third worked at full-time jobs for the entire year. As a point of reference, about two thirds of all men who had work experience in the same year worked full time the year round, while only one out of eight was a part-time worker.

Moreover, while it is true that there is considerable variation among industries with respect to the incidence of full-time, full-year employment of men. Table 6.2, which shows the frequency distribution of full-year, full-time employment and part-time employment for men and women by industry in

1964, indicates the much higher variability in full-time, full-year employment and part-time employment by industry for women than for men.

Table 6.2. *Percentage Distribution of Full-Time, Full-Year Workers and Part-Time Workers by Major Industry Group and Sex, 1964*

Percentage of full-time full-year workers	Percentage Distribution by Major Industry Groups	
	For Males	For Females
90 and over	2	0
80–90	8	0
70–80	14	3
60–70	7	4
50–60	4	10
40–50	2	6
30–40	0	5
20–30	2	4
10–20	2	0
0–10	1	0
Percentage of part-time workers		
0–5	17	5
5–10	10	9
10–15	5	2
15–20	2	1
20–25	3	5
25–30	0	2
30–35	0	3
35–40	2	1
40–45	0	1
45–50	0	2
50–55	0	1
55–60	0	0
60–65	0	2
65–70	0	1
70 and over	3	1

A similar picture emerges when variability of employment status, full time or part time, is compared by occupation for men and women.

Such widely differing experience for men on the one hand and women on the other suggests several questions, the most important of which concerns how the demand for labor and the supply of labor are differentiated by sex.

It is well to remind ourselves again that, while almost two out of every three females who had work experience during 1965 were in the peripheral labor force, only one out of three males with work experience was included in it. Even for those age groups of women where the percentage with work experience who worked full time the year round is highest—from 45 to 59—about 50 percent of the women in these age groups were peripheral workers, while among the age groups of males with work experience where the proportion of full-time, year-round workers was highest, the proportion of peripheral workers was only about 20 percent.

An even more radical contrast between the work experience of men and women is evident in the proportions of those with work experience who worked at part-time jobs. If we again confine our attention to the central age groups, we find that a negligible percentage of men had part-time work experience (3 percent or less for the age groups 25–34, 35–44, and 45–54), while the proportion of women in these age groups who had part-time work experience does not fall below 25 percent. It should be noted in this respect, however, that the proportions of those at the age extremes in both sexes whose work experience was part time becomes much more similar, particularly for youth.

If we turn to another aspect of peripheral work experience —intermittent rather than part-time work experience—we find once again marked differences between male and female patterns. In the central male age groups, only 3 percent of all men with full-time work experience during the year worked 26 weeks or less during 1965. On the other hand, intermittent or short-term work experience is relatively common for women. In the age group 25 to 34, for example, almost one fifth of women with full-time work experience actually worked 26 weeks or less. For the older age groups there is a pronounced tendency for workers with full-time work experience to work a longer portion of the year, but even in the age groups 35 to 44 and 45 to 54 about one woman in ten with full-time work experience worked 26 weeks or less. Moreover, a relatively large proportion of women of these age groups whose work experience was part time also worked 26 weeks or less. Again this is more common for the age group 25–34 than it is for the older age groups. Nevertheless, almost one half of all women 35 to 44 who had part-time work experience during 1965 worked 26 weeks or less.

When, therefore, we compare the total work experience of mature men and women, we find that we are confronted with gross differences: men overwhelmingly tend to be employed at full-time, full-year jobs whereas women are in fact divided into several major subgroups of which the full-time, full-year worker is the largest (approaching one half of all mature women with work experience); but among women we must also distinguish the part-time, full-year worker (about one tenth of all women with work experience), the part-time worker who works only part of the year (20 percent of all women with work experience), and, finally, the full-time worker who works part of the year.

How can we account for these broad differences between the work experience of men and women, taking into consideration at the same time the widely varying patterns that emerge in different occupations, industries, and age groups? One possible explanation is that these differences are simply the result of the different productivities in market and nonmarket activities of men and women, operating in conjunction with different attitudes toward leisure and different valuations of nonmarket productive activities as between the sexes. Such an explanation would emphasize that there may in fact be sufficient variability and flexibility in the employment opportunities generated by the economy with respect to both part-time and intermittent employment to allow the individual worker, whether male or female, to find his niche more or less freely. In this view differences in wage rates between full-time, part-time, and intermittent employment are the outcome of relatively unconstrained market forces and a sufficiently high degree of mobility between part-time and full-time employment at the margin.

If, following this line of thought, we were to assume that there was no difference between the attitudes of men and women toward leisure and income we could still account for part of the observed difference between male and female part-time employment if the net wage rate for men and women for similar occupations and in similar industries differed in a systematic fashion so that it was always lower for women than for men, even though nominal wage rates were the same for both men and women. If, for example, it was always necessary for a woman to pay an outsider to perform some of her household work if she accepted employment away from the home and if such payments never had to be made when a man worked away from the home, then net wages of women would be systematically lower than net wages of men. This might very well lead women to work fewer hours on the average than men. There are a number of other reasons why net wages of women, all costs of employment being taken into account including nonmonetary costs, might be lower than net wages of men for similar employment.

On the other hand, we might assume that net wages are more or less the same for men and women and then go on to account for the difference in employment patterns by asserting that women place a relatively higher valuation on leisure compared to income than men. The focus of our attention would then be placed upon those factors which might account for these male-female preference differences.

We might even go so far as to claim that there was a difference between the attitudes of men and women toward income and leisure which was rooted in some biological difference between the sexes or was the product of educational and cultural influences, men, for example, being systematically conditioned from their earliest years to a life of activity and creativity, women being as systematically conditioned toward passivity and receptivity, or, alternatively, men being systematically conditioned to get satisfaction from activities taking place outside the home, women on the other hand being conditioned to consider that domestic activities were the proper source of feminine satisfactions.

It seems appropriate at this point to note that differences in male and female work roles are, according to cultural anthropologists, extremely varied in the forms they take in particular societies. Although the biological differences between male and female may provide the initial basis for an individuation of work roles by sex, they by no means account for the actual roles that are assumed by men and women in particular societies. Margaret Mead has summed up the matter as follows:

The differences between the two sexes is one of the important conditions upon which we have built the many varieties of human culture that give human beings dignity and stature. In every known society, mankind has elaborated the biological division of labor into forms often very remotely related to the original biological differences that provided the original clues. Upon the contrast in bodily form and function, men have built analogies between sun and moon, night and day, goodness and evil, strength and tenderness, steadfastness and fickleness, endurance and vulnerability. Sometimes one quality has been assigned to one sex, sometimes to the other. Now it is boys who are thought of as infinitely vulnerable and in need of special cherishing care, now it is girls. In some societies it is girls for whom parents must collect a dowry or make husband-catching magic, in others the parental worry is over the difficulty of marrying off the boys. Some peoples think of women as too weak to work out of doors, others regard women as the appropriate bearers of heavy burdens, "because their heads are stronger than men's." . . . But we always find the patterning. We know of no culture that has said, articulately, that there is no difference between men and women except in the way they contribute to the creation of the next generation; that otherwise in all respects they are simply human beings with varying gifts. . . . However differently the traits have been assigned, some to one sex, some to the other, and some to both, however arbitrary the assignment must be seen to be (for surely it cannot be true that women's heads are both absolutely weaker—for carrying loads— and absolutely stronger—for carrying loads—than men's), although the division has been arbitrary, it has always been there in every society of which we have any knowledge.[1]

An interesting approach to one aspect of the peripheral work experience of women, the intermittent employment pattern, is provided by the work of Stuart Altman. Struck by the seasonal variations of gross entries of married women into the labor force, Altman observes that gross entries are relatively low and constant during the summer months and then rise abruptly in September, thereafter declining. A possible explanation of this labor force behavior, according to Altman, is that the low and constant levels of entries in the summer months are associated with the high marginal productivity of work in the household done by married women with children during the months of the year when children are not in school. The large volume of September entries is, according to this hypothesis, associated with the return of children to school

[1] Margaret Mead, *Male and Female: A Study of the Sexes in a Changing World* (New York: William Morrow & Company, 1949), pp. 7–8. Copyright 1949 by Margaret Mead.

and the consequent abrupt fall in the productivity of women in the home and the resulting increase in the relative attractiveness of paid employment outside the home. The underlying common sense of Altman's analysis is immediately apparent, but it has the further merit of being couched in terms of economic theory, particularly the opportunity cost of employment to married women, a cost which would seem to be subject to seasonal variation if the character of the family itself alters according to a seasonal pattern, particularly as children attend school.

A possible generalization of Altman's approach would lead us to examine whether there is a variation of the marginal productivity of women's work in the household which is associated with the pattern of weekly activities within the home or with the pattern of women's household work within the compass of the day. If such is the case, the peripheral work experience of some women would reflect such variations.

Moreover, we should be alert to the possibility that shifting patterns of parental responsibility for household tasks, shifts to which Margaret Mead calls attention in her *Male and Female*, may have provided the basis for radical changes in the marginal productivity of women within the home, particularly in its variability through the course of the day.[2] Similarly much of the impact of modern technology as it affects traditional homemaking tasks of women may have led to decreases in the time-specificity of parts of women's work. The home freezer, prepared foods, home laundries, clothes designed to be thrown away rather than repaired, all these developments act both to lower the amount of time required of women to perform basic homemaking functions and to free women from the necessity of performing many of them at a certain time of the day or on a certain day of the week.

[2] *Ibid.*, Parts III and IV.

YOUTH: THE PROCESS OF
COMMITMENT TO WORK

Young people, comprising in that term such diverse groups as teen-agers and young men and women in their early twenties, form a clearly distinguishable component of the peripheral work force. For the majority of youth the peripheral work experiences which they have during some portion of the years between 14 and 24 are part of the general process of exploration of the world of work and of discovery of the occupation, career, or industry to which they will eventually be more or less fully attached. But to others the work experiences (or lack of them) of these years are an important part of those influences which in sum tend to prevent a meaningful and complete attachment to work. Rather these work experiences lead to lack of clear career objectives, blunt or destroy whatever aspirations some young people have for the future, and confirm their belief, already perhaps strongly suggested by their environment and the experience of relatives and friends, that whatever the world of work may offer to others, it means for them at best a series of casual, intermittent, goalless jobs.

To young people, then, the meaning of these early work experiences differs widely. For some the income earned in part-time or summer work has little real significance to anyone except the young person himself, and for him the work is mainly a source of supplementary funds by means of which he can purchase items that promise to yield a very short term satisfaction. He performs work today in order to consume today, the whole transaction having a very short time dimension. At the other extreme is the teen-age girl or boy who works more or less regularly, even if only at part-time jobs or summer work, and whose time perspective is unusually long since the money earned is being accumulated for college and graduate school. In this case the actual work may seem casual and peripheral in the extreme but it is nevertheless an integral part of a very long term commitment to career and to eventual full-time work. Finally, for some young people work may provide part of the income which is essential for the maintenance of what, even with the addition of this income, is only at most a marginal standard of existence. Such a young person may be under considerable pressure from his family to explore all the part-time and full-time work possibilities open to him but his work experience may produce profound resentment on his part to a society where according to convention a young person is dependent upon his parents rather than the reverse.

These few remarks are merely to suggest how fraught with significance to future careers the work experience of the teen-ager and young adult may be and how varied is its meaning to the individual young person. At a time when unprecedented numbers of young people are entering a world of work which is rapidly changing its character and in which a large number of the traditional entry jobs are declining in relative, if not in absolute, size, those agencies which are responsible for the formation of manpower policy and those institutions which are responsible for carrying out whatever national and local policy our society has developed are confronted by a lack of systematic and reliable information about the transition period between peripheral work status and full-time status for various types of young people. The lack of such information hampers the development of relevant policy and its proper execution.

For all groups whose members are either more or less continually in the peripheral labor force or pass through it in the process of developing full-time work commitments or in retiring from work it would be highly desirable to have longitudinal studies in considerable depth. Several such studies are currently being carried out or are being developed, but in the absence of any large-scale investigation covering the last decade or so we are not able to discuss in detail the actual process a young person of a particular demographic character goes through as he develops the more or less permanent attitudes toward career and work commitment which will help to determine whether his working life is to be highly peripheral or not.

Lest it be thought, however, that it is the individual worker's attitudes which are the sole determinants of eventual work status, we should remind ourselves that employers on their side may well have in mind a typical set of work experiences (along with educational attainment) to which a young man who is to be considered for full-time, full-year work must to some extent conform. If the type of peripheral work experience which a young adult has already gone through is considered undesirable (too indicative, perhaps, of a casual attitude toward work as the employer sees it) he may be excluded from serious consideration for full-time, full-year status. Moreover, the employer may feel that the peripheral work experience of a young person may not have been conducive to the development of skills that are valuable in the kind of work which is generally full time the year round. If a considerable investment in on-the-job training of prospective full-time, full-year workers has to be made, the employer may search a candidate's previous work history carefully for clues to his stability and seriousness of purpose.

The importance of early work experience in determining the lifelong "set" of an individual toward work has long been noticed. In the latter part of the nineteenth century, for example, much of the concern felt in England over what were called the "wandering occupations"—the errand boys and girls, the street traders, and so forth (whose numbers apparently were astonishingly large)—was the product of the fear that these children, subject to erratic and casual employment, would turn into "lazy, shiftless and worthless men." [3] Indeed, a constant refrain of the nineteenth century, raised against any attempts to reduce the hours of work of young people, was that long hours and steady employment of very young people were essential if the new generation was to be inculcated with the value of unremitting industry.

In part because the employment of a vast number of children in highly visible work has ceased, in part because the existence of child labor laws has eased the community's conscience about the question of abuse of children in unhealthy, dangerous occupations and in cruelly long hours of employment, there seems to be nowadays only moderate general concern about the character of the employment experiences of young people. This does not mean that there is not acute concern about specific groups, for example the Negro teen-ager of Watts or the child of migratory workers. The general assumption, however, particularly among middle-class families whose children are apt to progress from high school to college, seems to be that work experience of young persons is a matter of relatively casual summer and after-school jobs which have little or no connection with the ultimate career of the individual, except as these work experiences are part of the general process of maturation. Work experience is considered to be desirable, it is true, but largely in order to accustom the young person to the discipline and rewards of work in general, rather than as part of the specific training and guidance which will lead to a lifelong attachment to a particular occupation or industry.

Such attitudes toward youthful work experience are of course entirely reasonable so long as post-high-school educational activity is considered to be the major determinant of eventual careers. The overwhelming importance of a success-

[3] Maurice W. Thomas, *Young People in Industry, 1750–1945* (London: Thomas Nelson and Sons, 1945), pp. 118, 136–51.

ful college and, more and more frequently, postgraduate educational experience to middle-class young people dwarfs whatever significance work experience during the years of adolescence might have to the great majority for the development of actual career commitments. Even for young people who may eventually end up as blue-collar workers and who may go no further educationally than the completion of high school, if that far, there appears to be surprisingly little continuity between the peripheral work experience of the adolescent and later attachment to industry and occupation. A study of the work history of younger employees of several large New York industrial firms by Marcia Freedman, for example, indicates the absence of any clear-cut line of development of work careers for many such young people.[4]

In the past decade concern has been expressed about the possibility that a concomitant of recent technological change has been the partial "drying up" of the types of jobs which in the past offered entry to the world of work to young people— the unskilled, blue-collar jobs provided by agriculture, construction, and the mass production industries requiring large numbers of relatively untrained operatives. The prospect of a decrease in the demand for such "entry workers," combined with an increase in the supply of such workers as a result of the rise in birth rates at the end of World War II, has, it is maintained by many observers, dangerous implications for the future. At its worst it seems to forebode a situation in which a central core of skilled workers—adult and for the most part white and male—have command over access to stable, highly paid employment, more and more white-collar and technical in character, while an increasing number of workers, young or nonwhite or female, or all simultaneously, swirl around the portals of industry, unable to penetrate the conventional

[4] Marcia Freedman, *The Process of Work Establishment* (New York: Columbia University Press, 1969).

"ports of entry," condemned to marginal work experiences, tempted to withdraw entirely from the labor force if, like Negro teen-agers, they are relatively more disadvantaged than their fellows. In this view of the labor market the labor force will become increasingly split into two groups—the permanently employed, highly paid technician who supervises the ever more automated firms and the permanently unemployed, increasingly supported by transfer payments from government. A larger and larger fraction of the new generation of potential workers, particularly those whose education is only average or less than average, can never, it is said, really expect to become fully attached to the world of work because the traditional method of approach, the lower-rung job, is in the process of collapsing and no substitute for it has been developed.

If this view of the way in which the younger worker enters the world of work is seriously at variance with the facts, if in fact he has usually become a worker through a series of exploratory ventures at employment, highly peripheral in character, then perhaps it would be appropriate to examine the peripheral work experiences of young people with greater care. It may indeed prove to be the case that changes in the character of peripheral work experience, changes in the ease of access to such experience, in the traditional progression of peripheral work experience, in the skills acquired and the attitudes formed by such experience, are as important for the development of future commitment to the labor force in general and to particular occupations and industries as changes in the character and quantity of the traditional blue-collar, full-time, full-year "entry type" jobs of the past.

PATTERNS OF YOUTH WORK EXPERIENCE

Table 6.3 summarizes the work experience in 1965 of young workers. As is to be expected, the percentage of the youngest age group, aged 14 to 17, that is involved in full-time, full-year work is trivial—only 1.5 of all those with work experience. On the other hand, one fifth of this group does work full time at some time during the year, the great majority 13 or less weeks a year. It should of course also be kept in mind that the labor force participation rate of this group is under 50 percent for boys and only just over 30 percent for girls.

The work experience, then, for this youngest group is overwhelmingly part time. Again the part-time experience is very apt to last much less than half of the year, almost 40 percent of both girls and boys working 13 or less weeks in a part-time job. However, it is worth noting that over one fifth of the boys in this group are attached to the world of work by part-time employment the year round. Only slightly more than one girl in ten has a similar work experience.

Turning to the age group 18–19, it should be noted that only about one out of seven, either male or female, works full time the full year. About a third of this age group, somewhat more for females, slightly less for males, works more than 35 hours a week, but for a half year or less. It is interesting to note that a higher percentage of girls than boys works 35 hours or more a week, although a slightly smaller percentage works a full year. Part-time employment the year round is more common among boys than girls in this age group, more than one in ten boys having this experience, only about one in twenty girls. On the other hand, a slightly larger percentage of girls than boys (more than one out of five in both cases) works part time for a half year or less. The semi-attached character of this age group to the world of work is very evident.

The age group 20 to 24 has made only a partial transition to adult work patterns. This is particularly the case for males. The pattern for females in this age group differs only in one or two important aspects from that of older women. The pattern for young men of this age group, however, is markedly different in almost all aspects from the pattern which will mark the balance of their working experience as a group.

Table 6.3. *Percentage Distribution of Work Experience of Younger Workers by Sex and Age, 1965*

			Weeks of Work Experience					
Hours	*Age Group*	*13 or Less*	*14–26*	*27–39*	*40–47*	*48–49*	*50–52*	*Total*
Male								
Full time	14–17	16.0	3.0	1.1	0.3		1.8	22.2
	18–19	20.0	11.1	6.1	2.9	1.2	14.9	56.2
	20–24	9.0	8.1	7.6	6.3	4.1	52.1	87.1
Part time	14–17	32.5	13.2	6.1	2.3	1.0	22.7	77.8
	18–19	11.9	9.7	5.6	1.9	1.4	13.3	43.8
	20–24	2.4	2.2	1.4	1.0	0.5	5.5	12.9
Total	14–17	48.5	16.2	7.2	2.6	1.0	24.5	100.0
	18–19	31.9	20.8	11.7	4.8	2.6	28.2	100.0
	20–24	11.4	10.3	9.0	7.3	4.6	57.6	100.0
Female								
Full time	14–17	9.5	3.0	0.9	0.2	0.1	1.2	14.8
	18–19	21.6	18.2	7.5	2.5	1.3	14.5	65.5
	20–24	13.2	13.2	9.1	5.7	3.1	38.5	82.7
Part time	14–17	45.1	17.9	5.7	3.1	1.6	11.8	85.2
	18–19	13.7	8.2	4.0	2.1	0.9	5.5	34.5
	20–24	6.4	4.1	2.1	1.1	0.7	2.9	17.3
Total	14–17	54.6	20.9	6.6	3.3	1.7	13.0	100.0
	18–19	35.3	26.4	11.5	4.6	2.2	20.0	100.0
	20–24	19.6	17.2	11.2	6.8	3.8	41.4	100.0

	Percent with Work Experience	
Age Group	*Male*	*Female*
14–17	49.1	43.6
18–19	85.5	74.3
20–24	92.4	97.7

This is most clearly demonstrated by the percentage of the age group which is attached to work on a full-time, full-year basis. Although the percentage of the group has risen from the

14.9 percent which characterizes the 18–19 age group, it is still only slightly above 50 percent (52.1), far below the 81.9 percent that is attained by the 25–54 age group. (It should be noted that a finer breakdown of this latter group would show even higher percentage rates being attained by workers in the 35–44 and 45–54 age groups—84.1 and 82.5 respectively.) Again for purposes of comparison it should be noted that if those workers who work 48–49 weeks were added to the group working 50–52 weeks as being for all practical purposes full-year workers, seven out of eight males in the 35–44 age group are full-year, full-time workers. It should also be noted that the major jumps to full-time status are made from the 14.9 percentage of the 18–19 age group to the 52.1 percentage of the 20–24 age group and from there to the 78.8 percentage of the 25–34 age group.

THE NONWHITE WORKER: PERIPHERAL WORK EXPERIENCE AS AN ASPECT OF DISCRIMINATORY PRACTICES

TRANSFORMATIONS IN NEGRO LIFE EXPERIENCE, 1900–1960

The nonwhite worker is particularly subject to peripheral work experience. Moreover, Negroes, who constitute some 90 percent of the statistical group which is labeled "nonwhite," are much more likely to be subject to whatever disadvantages such work experience entails for the adult worker, particularly the adult male, than are the other major groups who, together with the Negro, make up the "nonwhite" category, largely the Chinese and the Japanese. These latter two groups are less affected by peripherality in work experience than the population in general, if educational attainment, occupation, and other characteristics can be taken to indicate patterns of stability. The American Indian is also included among "nonwhites," but his work experience is so special that it deserves separate treatment. The Mexican-American, a member of another minority group, is still to a large extent a farm worker, though increasingly an urban resident. Finally, another large minority group, the Puerto Ricans in such large urban areas as New York, is exposed to somewhat the same kind of peripheral work experience that the urban Negro faces.

Within the space of some sixty to seventy years the life experience of the Negro in the United States has been subject to a number of profound changes. Many of these changes bear upon his susceptibility to peripheral work experience, determining, if not the extent, at least the particular type of peripheral work he performs. In 1900 approximately 90 percent of all Negroes in the United States lived in the South where they constituted one third of the population and were largely rural. (Statistics involving the Negro in the South at this time must be assumed to be nothing more than approximations since it is certain that enumeration of Negroes in censuses was carried out in the most haphazard fashion, particularly, it would seem, in the rural regions with which we are concerned.) In the rest of the United States Negroes constituted approximately 2 percent of the population; in the western states as a whole they numbered only 30,000 in the year 1900. By 1950 the Negro was among the most urban of the major demographic groups that compose the American society and he was almost as apt to be found in the North and West as in the South, some 40 percent of all Negroes in that year living in regions other than the South. In 1960 the Negro still constituted, it is true, a large proportion of the total population of the South, some 25 percent of the total, but in a number of states of the North, particularly in the Middle Atlantic and East North Central areas, he made up about one tenth of the total population, reaching much higher proportions in the larger central cities.

Moreover, the age distribution of the Negro underwent similar remarkable changes over the first half of the twentieth century. In 1900 approximately 70 percent of the 8.8 million Negroes in the United States were under 30 years of age; in 1950 only 55 percent of the 15 million Negroes were in this age group. In 1900 less than 5 percent of the Negroes were 60 years or older; in 1950 the figure had risen to more than 8 percent and the absolute size of this part of the Negro population had grown from about four hundred thousand in 1900 to about one and a quarter million in 1950. In comparison, however, it should be noted that in 1950 almost 14 percent of the white population was at least 60 years of age!

Finally these same years saw a remarkable change in the educational attainment of the Negro. In 1900 the schooling of the southern Negro frequently consisted of little more than a few months' attendance over a period of a few years in school which scarcely pretended to educate the Negro child. It seems certain that even the tragically low levels of recorded educational attainment of most southern Negroes do not give more than an impression of the failure of the South to give even minimum literacy to the great majority of Negroes. Moreover, the life experience, particularly the work experience, of the Negro in the rural South was calculated to erase whatever beginnings of literacy the schools might have achieved. Exposed to no newspapers, far from any libraries, only occasionally in contact with even small-town influences, a large number of rural Negroes were, not surprisingly, functionally illiterate.

By the 1960s the Negro had made remarkable strides in his efforts to achieve educational parity with the rest of the population. In the sixty years between 1890 and 1950, for example, it is estimated that the proportion of Negroes who were illiterate fell from 57 percent to slightly more than 10 percent. Such estimates are necessarily imprecise; perhaps more revealing are data on median years of schooling completed. Taking age groups in 1950, we find the following differences in schooling:

Median Years of Schooling
Completed

Age Group	Nonwhite	White
25–29	8.4	12.4
30–34	7.8	11.9
35–39	7.1	10.7
40–44	6.5	9.9
45–49	6.0	8.9
50–54	5.6	8.7
55–59	5.1	8.5
60–64	4.7	8.3
65–69	4.0	8.2

Negroes who were educated in the 1890s tended to receive less than five years of schooling if the experience of survivors who went to school in that decade is a fair indication. On the other hand, white children, it would seem, were already receiving on the average more than eight years of schooling.

Table 6.4. *Median School Years Completed by Whites and Nonwhites, by Residence, 1965*

	Male		Female	
	White	Nonwhite	White	Nonwhite
Total	12.2	10.0	12.3	11.1
Nonfarm	12.3	10.3	12.4	11.2
U.S., excluding the South	12.3	11.1	12.4	12.0
South	12.1	9.1	12.3	10.1
Farm	9.4	6.1	12.1	8.5

Source: *The Negroes in the United States: Their Economic and Social Situation*, Bureau of Labor Statistics Bulletin No. 1511, June, 1966.

Turning to the educational attainment of Negroes in the very recent past, we possess a wealth of data which shows both the very great recent advances made by Negroes and the residual effects of inadequate schooling in the past. Table 6.4

gives median school years completed for whites and nonwhites in the labor force by residence. It is important to keep in mind that the table presents data only for members of the labor force. Confining our attention to this group, we can observe that the nonwhite worker, with the exception of those in the South and on farms (Negro farmers are almost exclusively southern and seem to suffer an educational deficiency which is in part derived from their southern location, in part from their occupational character), has come close to obtaining parity with white members of the labor force, at least according to the rough measure given by school years completed. It is unfortunately probably true that the quality of schooling of the nonwhite is below that of the white population, but in the nature of the case it is not possible to make any precise estimates of the difference in quality.

However, when we turn to statistics of school years completed by those who are not members of the labor force, and not in school, we find a very different situation. For whites the number of school years completed by male nonmembers of the labor force is astonishingly low in comparison with the rest of the white population. The median for such males is below 9 years. No such difference emerges from the figures of white females not in the labor force compared with those who are members of the labor force. From the point of view of the nonwhite population, the same wide differentials exist between labor force members and nonmembers in median school years completed, but in the case of nonwhite nonmembers of the labor force the median years completed are so few, 7.1 for the country as a whole, as to suggest that a major part of the explanation of the fact that many members of this group are not in the labor force is their marked educational deficiency.

From the point of peripheral work experience, the rapid

changes that have taken place in the educational attainment of the nonwhite American in the last few decades are particularly significant. In sum, the nonwhite population, to a much greater extent than the white population, is characterized by very wide differentials in educational attainment by region and age which tend to divide the total nonwhite population into a number of subgroups. First of all, the younger Negro tends to have a much higher educational attainment relative to older Negroes than does his white counterpart. Moreover, the quality of this education may be as different as the quantity. The great majority of older Negroes were educated in the South and in rural areas. A large proportion of Negro youth have been and are being educated in urban areas, increasingly in the North. Second, the Negro worker in the South is at a greater educational disadvantage relative to the northern non-white worker than is his white counterpart. If peripheral work experience tends to bear more heavily in certain industries and occupations on those who are educationally at a disadvantage, we should expect to find that the older Negro, and particularly the older southern Negro, is much more likely to find that peripheral work constitutes an important part of his work life.

WORK EXPERIENCE OF THE NONWHITE

Ideally the work experience of the nonwhite worker should be compared with that of the white worker in all of the dimensions that have been explored so far: by sex, age, occupation, and industry.

The available data, however, do not provide a breakdown of nonwhite employment patterns which would allow the construction of the simple matrices which were used in Chapter III to present the gross patterns of work experience involving part-year and part-time employment. It is nevertheless possible to construct a matrix from information given in Special Labor Force Report No. 76 (see Table 6.5).

Table 6.5. *Percentage Distribution of Work Experience of Whites and Nonwhites, 1965*

Weeks Worked	White	Nonwhite
Full time (35 hours and more)		
1–26	10.2	13.3
27–49	12.6	16.0
50–52	57.2	47.4
Part time (less than 35 hours		
1–52	19.9	23.2

Source: Special Labor Force Report No. 76, *Work Experience of the Population in 1965* (Washington, D.C.: U.S. Department of Labor, Bureau of Labor Statistics), Table A-8.

The pronounced differentials in favor of white workers in terms of full-time, full-year attachment to work are evident in every cell of this very truncated matrix. Unfortunately the data upon which Table 6.5 is based do not permit a distinction by weeks worked for part-time workers. It seems probable that the pattern which emerges in the case of full-time workers would be reproduced in the case of part-time workers, namely that the nonwhite worker tends to be concentrated more heavily in those cells representing less than full-year employment. To discover whether the differences in the above matrix are produced by differences in white-nonwhite employment experiences which are sex linked, the two matrices in Table 6.6 compare white-nonwhite experience by sex.

Both male and female nonwhite workers have markedly lower rates of full-time, full-year employment experience. However, there are significant differences in the white-nonwhite differentials which emerge when patterns for males are compared with patterns for females. Nonwhite males fall short of white males by almost 11 percentage points in rates of full-time, full-year employment experience. In contrast to this wide differential, nonwhite females fall short of white females in this category by less than five percentage points. While more than two out of three white male workers are employed full time the full year, slightly less than six out of ten nonwhite males are in this category.

Table 6.6 *Percentage Distribution of Work Experience by Sex and Color, 1965*

Weeks Worked	Male		Female	
	White	Nonwhite	White	Nonwhite
Full time (35 hours and more)				
1–26	7.2	10.1	15.1	17.3
27–49	11.6	16.3	14.2	15.7
50–52	68.4	57.6	39.3	34.9
Part time (less than 35 hours)				
1–52	12.8	16.0	31.4	32.1

Similarly the difference between part-time white and nonwhite rates is less marked for females than for males. The rate for nonwhite male workers is almost a third higher than for white male workers, while the rate for nonwhite female workers in this category is only slightly higher than for white female workers. As in so many dimensions of employment experience, the nonwhite male worker is in a relatively weaker position than the nonwhite female when compared with white male and female workers.

It is possible to compare white-nonwhite employment experiences by a number of other dimensions, one important one being age groups. In the youngest age group, 14 to 19, both white males and females and nonwhite males have rather similar work experience, with nonwhites being somewhat more engaged in full-time work, even though the great bulk of it is full time for less than half a year. While almost two out of three whites in this age group work only part-time schedules, less than 60 percent of nonwhite males work at part-time jobs.

It is the nonwhite girl aged 14 to 19 whose experience is markedly different from that of others in this age group. Although she is much more apt to be a full-time worker than is a white girl (and more apt to be a full-time worker than either a white or nonwhite male), the percentage of nonwhite girls who work full time for a half year or less is far above the rates for nonwhite males and both male and female white youngsters. It should be noted also that the percentage of nonwhite girls who have work experience is very much lower than either white males or females or nonwhite males. Where white and nonwhite males in this age group have work experience rates in the neighborhood of 50 percent or above (white males rather higher in fact), only one of three nonwhite girls in this age group has work experience during the course of the year. This very low rate relative to other members of this age group may indicate a profound generational change because it is not in evidence in the next age group, 20–24, and for the very large group 25–64 the work experience rate of nonwhite females is far above that of white females.

The evidence suggests very strongly that the nonwhite girl in this age group is in fact exposed to a series of relatively short-term jobs, albeit full time. Only one in ten nonwhite girls has a job that lasts as long as half a year, although four out of ten work at full-time jobs sometime during the year. Since it is quite probable that any youngster who seeks full-time employment at this age has more at stake than do those who are willing to settle for part-time employment, it may indeed be a most discouraging experience for the nonwhite girl (discouraging to the extent that it may help to explain also the relatively low labor force participation rate) to find that full-time employment is often a casual affair. And of course the quality of full-time jobs which are so easily terminated probably leaves much to be desired.

If we turn to the next age group, those between 20 and 24 years old, again it is noteworthy that the gross rates for white and nonwhite males are very similar. If we were to take as a subgroup those whose education was already terminated, these relatively encouraging results would not be so evident, simply because a much higher percentage of white males in this age group are engaged in college or graduate school work and students generally prefer part-time employment.

Only about one out of eight males in this age group, white or nonwhite, is employed at a part-time job. While more nonwhite than white males find that their full-time jobs last between 26 and 49 weeks, more white males, one out of five, are employed full time 26 weeks or less, probably reflecting the large numbers of college students who take full-time employment during the summer vacation.

For all four subgroups of the 20–24 age group, white and nonwhite males and females, the process of increasing commitment to full-time work experience is very much in evidence. However, there is a curious difference between the experience of nonwhite girls in this age group and that of nonwhite girls in the younger group. Whereas nonwhite girls aged 14 to 19 had by far the lowest rates of part-time work experience, nonwhite girls in the 20–24 age group had a rate of part-time work experience 50 percent higher than that of white girls and double that of white and nonwhite males. If this represents a disadvantaged attachment to work, the disadvantage may be reflected in the very much smaller rate of participation in full-time, full-year work. Where almost four out of ten white girls in this age group are working full time the full year, only 30 percent of nonwhite girls have work experience of this character. Almost a third of the nonwhite girls are employed full time for less than half a year.

For the work force as a whole it is probably more significant to compare the nonwhite-white experience for that great bloc of workers who are between 25 and 64 years old.

How do the other three groups—white female, nonwhite male, and nonwhite female—measure up to the standard set by white males?

Table 6.7. *Percentage Distribution of Employment Experience of White and Nonwhite Males, Aged 25-64, 1965*

	(1) White Males	(2) Nonwhite Males	(1) — (2)
Full time			
50–52 weeks	81.9	69.6	+12.3
27–49 weeks	11.9	17.6	— 5.7
1–26 weeks	3.2	5.9	— 2.7
Part time	3.0	7.1	— 4.1

Comparing, first, white males with nonwhite males, we arrive at the figures shown in Table 6.7. It should be noted at the outset that the work experience rate of nonwhite males in the age group 25–64 is below that of white males, 92.3 as opposed to 95.6, and it is possible, though of course by its very nature difficult to assess how much, that the reported nonwhite work experience rate is a good deal above actual work experience because of the possibly large statistical undercount of nonwhite males.

It is evident that the nonwhite male's typical employment experience tends to be much more strongly characterized by either short-term, full-time employment or part-time employment. More than four out of five white males aged 25 to 64 are employed at full-time, full-year jobs; only two thirds of nonwhite males of these ages have this type of employment. A negligible amount of white males are employed at part-time jobs; one in every fourteen Negro males between 25 and 64 was so employed in 1965.

Again only a very small percentage of white males in this age group are employed half the year or less at full-time jobs. For the nonwhite male this is a fairly common work experience involving about one in fifteen. And to weight the situation of the nonwhite even more adversely against him if full-time, full-year employment is the desideratum, the lower work experience rates for nonwhites and the problem of the uncounted nonwhites should always be borne in mind. A certain number—6.5 percent of nonwhites in this age group are not in the labor force—represent individuals who have withdrawn from the labor force because of chronic difficulty in finding employment, physical disability, and other reasons. Some of these individuals should be considered peripheral. In addition, some of the uncounted are certainly peripheral workers, although in this case it is not possible to say just what the employment experience of the uncounted really is. It is safe to assume, however, that many persons in the uncounted group represent the most detached members of society, their detachment extending to work (indeed it may in large part spring from a preexisting weakness of attachment to work).

Table 6.8. *Percentage Distribution of Employment Experience of White and Nonwhite Females, Aged 25–64, 1965*

	(1) White Females	(2) Nonwhite Females	(1) − (2)
Full time			
50–52 weeks	46.4	41.2	+5.2
27–49 weeks	15.4	17.7	−2.3
1–26 weeks	11.3	12.5	−1.2
Part time	26.8	28.6	−1.8

A comparison of white female and nonwhite female employment experience for this age group reveals much the same patterns of differentials (see Table 6.8). However, it is noteworthy that the differentials in favor of white women are much smaller than in the case of white men. And because adult women in general are much less likely to work full time, the typical nonwhite female worker in this age group is much more apt to have work experience which, in so far as the length of the work week and the length of the work year are concerned, fits into prevailing white patterns. Her disadvantages are very real: she is less likely to have a full-time, full-year job and more likely to work part time. But in a gross sense the differences are not as extreme as in the case of the nonwhite male worker, perhaps another indication of the relatively weak position that the nonwhite male worker has, not only within the predominant white patterns, but within the nonwhite group as well. And of course any discussion of white and nonwhite female work experiences for this broad age band would be out of touch with reality if it did not take into account the very marked difference in work experience rates between the two groups. Whereas nonwhite male work experience rates are lower than white male rates for this age group, quite the reverse is true for females. Almost two out of three nonwhite women are members of the labor force; only very slightly more than half of white women are members.

Table 6.9. *Percentage Distribution of Employment Experience of White and Nonwhite Males, Aged 65 and Over, 1965*

	(1) White Males	(2) Nonwhite Males	(1) — (2)
Full time			
50–52 weeks	44.3	31.4	+12.9
27–49 weeks	9.6	14.5	— 4.9
1–26 weeks	9.6	9.5	+ 0.1
Part time	36.6	44.5	— 7.9

A final age group to be examined is the category of those 65 years and older. Again there is a noticeable difference between white and nonwhite patterns, and a marked increase in the gap seems evident (see Table 6.9). Female workers in this age group show a pattern of differentials in favor of full-time, full-year employment patterns for whites as opposed to nonwhites (see Table 6.10). One peculiarity that emerges from Table 6.10 is that nonwhite women of this age group have shifted overwhelmingly to a part-time status, some two thirds of them working on such a basis, while only slightly more than half of all white women are similarly occupied. The work experience rates of the previous age group, 25 to 64, are again reflected for women workers in the group 65 and over; although the rate is quite low, the higher rate of participation for nonwhites is maintained.

Table 6.10. *Percentage Distribution of Employment Experience of White and Nonwhite Females, Aged 65 and Over, 1965*

	(1) White Females	(2) Nonwhite Females	(1) − (2)
Full time			
50–52 weeks	29.3	16.2	+13.1
27–49 weeks	8.5	12.0	− 3.5
1–26 weeks	10.4	7.8	+ 2.6
Part time	51.8	64.1	−12.3

A theoretical point of some interest may emerge from the above tables. It can be roughly put as follows: nonwhite women have high rates of full-time work experience at short-lived jobs in the younger age groups. Work experience for some of this group in fact takes the form of multiple job holding, each job being only part-time employment and the total hours worked per week being less than 35, therefore placing the worker in the part-time category. Although such a worker has given up an effort to achieve full-time work status, she does so in an effort to minimize the risks involved in intermittent full-time employment. It may still be true that any one of her part-time jobs may be terminated abruptly, but not all of them are apt to be terminated at the same time. And it also may be true that the psychic costs of finding part-time employment and losing part-time employment are much less than the psychic costs of being hired or fired from a full-time job. The importance given to just this element of the costliness (in an emotional sense) of the job-search experience is emphasized by Lloyd Reynolds in his *Structure of Labor Markets*. Being hired or fired from a full-time job may very well be a much more consequential act than the experience of being hired or fired from a part-time job. Therefore the latter may more easily be accepted by groups to whom being fired from a full-time job that has raised high expectations may become cumulatively harder to bear each additional time it is experienced.

THE OLDER WORKER

THE PROCESS OF DISENGAGEMENT

Part-time and intermittent work experience is a characteristic pattern of activity of a large number of older workers. At the same time we find that many older workers have a firmer attachment to particular occupations and industries than do many younger workers. This strong commitment manifests itself in the relatively long tenure of many older workers. The obverse of long tenure, however, seems to be longer spells of unemployment for many older workers than for younger workers, spells the length of which tends to encourage withdrawal from the labor force entirely in some cases.

Attachment to the labor force itself declines, it should be noted, at first rather slowly with increasing age, then precipitously. In 1965, for example, the labor force participation rate for white males aged 45 to 54 years was 96 percent, but for white males 55 to 64 years old the rate was only 85 percent and for the oldest age group, 65 and over, it was only 28 percent. The rate for women aged 45 to 54 was 50 percent, declining to 40 percent for the age group 55–64, and falling to just under 10 percent for the oldest age group. A similar pattern is displayed by nonwhite older age groups. It should be borne in mind, moreover, that the labor force participation rates of older male workers, particularly those over 65, have been falling rapidly since the end of World War II. Rates for women in the age group 55 to 64 have on the contrary increased over this period of time quite markedly—from 23 percent for white females in 1948 to 40 percent in 1965 and from 38 percent for nonwhite females in 1948 to 49 percent in 1965. Participation rates for women 65 and over have not changed to any noticeable extent, particularly in the last ten years.

There has been considerable discussion of the effect of institutional factors, centered particularly upon social security pension regulations and retirement policies of private and public employers, as such policies bear upon labor force participation rates of older workers and, in the case of social security, upon part-time employment. By setting differential penalties upon employment of differing duration, reaching the level of a 100 percent tax on earnings above a certain amount long before the usual worker 65 or over has been employed for a full-time, full-year period, social security regulations undoubtedly encourage some workers to engage in peripheral work experiences who would otherwise perhaps be inclined to remain in the labor force in a full-time, full-year status.

On the other hand, retirement policies of most private companies and most governmental agencies place an abrupt and final limit to full-time employment in occupations and industries to which many workers have devoted the greater part of their adult life, forcing the individual worker who wishes to continue gainful employment to explore new and in many cases peripheral employment areas.

It would, however, be misleading to imply that part-time employment of most older workers is the result of various constraints placed upon them by rigid institutional regulations. On the contrary, it is probable that for a large number of older workers part-time or intermittent employment experience is an essential element in the process of disengagement from the world of work, lessening to an important degree the economic and emotional shock which would result from a sudden cessation of all work activity.

This process of disengagement from the world of work on a mass scale is a relatively new phenomenon in human history and all too little is known about it. Indeed, until life expectancies for men and women promised a substantial number of years of retirement most workers terminated their actual life and their work life at roughly the same time, epidemic illnesses carrying many workers off in the prime of life. In addition, the problem of the superannuated worker in agriculture has always been substantially different from the problem facing the urban industrial and commercial employee. It was often possible for an elderly farmer to slacken off both effort and hours in a gradual fashion, particularly where sons could take over the farm. Where this was not possible, it is probable that the elderly farmer simply overworked himself in an effort to keep his farm operating. We can perhaps appreciate the importance of two factors, short life expectancies and the predominantly rural character of the labor force in earlier periods of our history, if we recall the following circumstances. In 1850 the life expectancy of a newborn male child in Massachusetts (probably as high as any state in that year) was 38 years. As late as 1900 life expectancy for the white male child was only 46 years and for the nonwhite male child it was less than 33 years! In contrast, the white male child born in 1955 could expect to live 67 years, the nonwhite male child 61 years. And the change in life expectancies of female children over this same period was even more spectacular, from 49 to 73 years for white children, from 34 years to 66 for nonwhites.

In 1850 almost five out of eight workers were engaged in agriculture. By 1900 the proportion had fallen to slightly more than one out of three workers. By 1965 the agricultural worker constituted only about one out of every sixteen employed persons. The farm as a place to terminate a working life ceased to be really significant between 1900 and 1960. The problem of peripheral work experience for the elderly is predominantly a problem for the urban industrial society of our own day. The character of such work experience also differs in a number of essential ways from much of the peripheral work experience of other major groups of the labor force.

In the first place, and perhaps most significantly, part-time and intermittent work experience for the older worker is in the great majority of cases, particularly for the white male worker, a type of work experience which follows upon rather firm commitment to the world of work, most of the white male workers having previously worked, as already noticed, full-time, full-year schedules. Unfortunately, for many of these full-time, full-year workers the very industries and occupations which provide the firmest basis for full commitment of the worker during his prime years are the areas of the economy and the kinds of occupations which tend to offer the fewest opportunities for peripheral work.

Secondly, peripheral work for the older worker is frequently associated with decreasing physical capacity and with obsolescence of the skills which provided the basis of his full-time, full-year employment in the past. Moreover, the industry or occupation to which the aging worker has been attached is more likely to be among the less dynamic areas of the economy the longer he has been attached to it. Both the worker and his industry or occupation may simultaneously be entering that part of the life cycle in which retraction is forced upon them.

Finally it is important to keep in mind that the economic situation of the older worker is itself very much a product of his previous work experience. If he has been a full-time, full-year worker in an industry producing durable goods and characterized by a strong union structure, for example, he may have not only the maximum pension provided by social security but a substantial pension from his union or his company as well, to which he can add in a good number of cases substantial savings accumulated over a lifetime of steady work. Moreover, in some companies, Eastman Kodak being a conspicuous example, he may find himself part of a highly organized and active group of retired workers, provided either by his company or by his union with a rather full set of services designed to make his retirement as pleasant as possible.

On the other hand, those workers whose attachment to the work force has been most peripheral throughout the central years of their working life are most apt to enter the period of withdrawal from the labor force due to increasing age with the fewest resources and the smallest pensions. Moreover, they often have the fewest and weakest supportive agencies and institutions, in the form of old age programs of unions, churches, and companies or in the form of a stable family structure, to rely upon. One noteworthy exception, however, is the married woman who entered the labor force to supplement the earnings of a husband employed full time the full year. One of her objectives may have been to assist in the accumulation of sufficient family savings to make possible the complete retirement of her husband and herself when his working life is ended.

Research on the characteristics of the older worker, particularly on the experience of the older worker who is in the process of withdrawing from the work force, is obviously of increasing importance, if only because the number of such workers is bound to increase in the future. (The percentage of individuals aged 65 and over increased from 4.1 to 9.1 in the United States between 1900 and 1965.) Important light will be thrown upon this subject when the study presently being conducted by a research group at Ohio State University on the older worker is completed. This longitudinal investigation, covering a period of five years, will make it possible to correlate work experience over the last years of working life with a number of demographic and other variables.

Investigations of the process of disengagement from the world of work also owe a very large debt to the work of Lowell Gallaway for the Social Security Administration. In his monograph *The Retirement Decision*, Gallaway explicitly applies "the tools of formal economic analysis to the research problems that abound in the social insurance area." In the introduction to his monograph, Gallaway presents a succinct statement of the complexity of the "retirement decision" and at the same time points out the contribution which economic theory can make to the analysis:

The enlarged concern for the condition of our older citizens has stimulated research in a number of areas of inquiry. In particular, much has been done with respect to increasing our knowledge of the medical, psychological, sociological, and economic problems associated with increasing age. All of these factors are of importance in understanding the behavior of older members of the society, for they all have a significant impact on the one decision which more than anything else summarizes the various facets of the problems of aging, viz., the "retirement" decision. . . . Quite obviously, what we have here called the "retirement" decision is a peculiarly complex choice situation, for it must, perforce, encompass a variety of considerations. The physical health of the worker, his subjective appreciation of the physical difficulties of continuing work, his psychological attitudes towards work and retirement, the attitudes of the culture in which he lives towards work and retirement, the availability of work opportunities, the degree of remuneration for available work opportunities, and the availability of nonwork types of retirement income all influence an individual's decision as to what extent he should modify his past pattern of work activities.[5]

Against this background of multiple and interrelated general factors which impinge upon the individual worker during the period of disengagement from the world of work, Gallaway points out that economic theory can

provide a systematic basis for framing hypotheses suitable for empirical investigation, and . . . indicate the inter-relationships between the economic phenomena under discussion and the other factors influencing the retirement decision.[6]

The body of his monograph is devoted to a theoretical discussion, resting primarily on the application of the tools of indifference analysis of consumer decision-making to the retirement decision. Indifference maps which relate income and leisure are used to present the three possibilities of choice facing the older worker: full retirement, partial retirement, and full work. Gallaway then tests a number of hypotheses about the retirement decision and concludes by presenting some estimates of the economic impact of the OASDI retirement benefit provisions on labor force participation of older workers.

PATTERNS OF PERIPHERAL WORK EXPERIENCE
OF OLDER WORKERS

As in the case of young workers, it is a matter of judgment where the line should be drawn which will isolate the "older

[5] Lowell Gallaway, *The Retirement Decision: An Exploratory Essay*, Research Report No. 9, U.S. Department of Health, Education, and Welfare (Washington, D.C.: Government Printing Office, 1965), p. 1.
[6] *Ibid.*, p. 2.

worker" as a group. In the case of young workers the age group from 20 to 24 seems to be clearly transitional in character, markedly different in behavior from the age groups between 24 and 54, but no such clear-cut dividing line can be found for older workers until the conventional retirement age of 65 is reached.

However, a useful boundary may be that between workers under 60 and those 60 and over. This is because there is a clear downturn in male full-time, full-year rates, a downturn which in fact begins in the 45–54 age group but finally in the case of the 60–64 age group carries the rate below that achieved by the 25–34 age group. The rate then decreases quite rapidly for succeeding groups so that, for the group over 70 years old, only about 35 percent of males with work experience are working full time the full year, while the rate for females has fallen to about 20 percent. (It should again be borne in mind that work experience rates taper off very rapidly for both men and women after they reach 60 years of age; by the time they are 70 or over, the rate for men is down to 23 percent and that for women is below 10 percent.)

A marked characteristic of older workers, the gradual but increasing rate at which they shift from full-time to part-time work as they get older, is revealed by Table 6.11. In the age group 65–69, one male worker out of ten is already working part time for the whole year and this rate increases to almost one in five for the age group 70 and over. At the same time there is a very marked increase in the number of workers, both male and female, who work only part of the year at part-time jobs. In the 65–69 age group about one male worker out of seven is attached to work in this loose fashion while one out of five women has a similar relation to work. In the age group 70 and over, one out of five male and female workers works less than half a year at a part-time job, the great majority of them working 13 weeks or less.

Table 6.11. *Percentage Distribution of Work Experience of Older Workers by Sex and Age, 1965*

Hours	Age Group	13 or Less	14–26	27–39	40–47	48–49	50–52	Total
Male								
Full time	55–59	1.5	2.7	5.2	4.8	2.9	78.1	95.1
	60–64	1.9	2.4	4.9	5.4	2.6	72.5	90.5
	65–69	4.9	5.5	6.5	3.7	1.9	49.2	71.7
	70+	5.0	3.4	3.1	2.6	1.4	34.9	50.5
Part time	55–59	0.8	1.0	0.9	0.3		1.9	4.9
	60–64	1.9	2.4	0.8	0.4	0.3	3.7	9.5
	65–69	7.3	5.7	2.4	1.5	0.8	10.5	28.3
	70+	13.2	7.5	3.7	3.1	1.3	20.7	49.5
Total	55–59	2.3	3.7	6.1	5.1	2.9	80.0	100.0
	60–64	3.8	4.8	5.7	5.8	2.9	76.2	100.0
	65–69	12.2	11.2	8.9	5.2	2.7	59.7	100.0
	70+	18.2	10.9	6.8	5.7	2.7	55.6	100.0
Female								
Full time	55–59	4.2	3.1	7.4	6.2	2.5	52.3	75.7
	60–64	3.8	3.9	8.4	5.8	2.2	47.6	71.8
	65–69	4.5	5.5	4.9	3.2	1.2	30.9	50.1
	70+	5.4	4.9	4.7	2.9	0.8	23.8	42.5
Part time	55–59	4.3	3.3	2.5	1.5	0.5	12.2	24.3
	60–64	5.7	3.1	2.1	3.2	1.0	13.0	28.2
	65–69	13.6	7.8	6.7	4.1	1.8	15.9	49.9
	70+	13.5	7.2	6.0	5.0	2.1	23.8	57.5
Total	55–59	8.5	6.4	9.9	7.7	3.0	64.4	100.0
	60–64	9.5	7.0	10.5	9.0	3.2	60.6	100.0
	65–69	18.1	13.3	11.6	7.3	3.0	46.8	100.0
	70+	18.9	12.1	10.7	7.9	2.9	47.6	100.0

CONCLUSION

This presentation of the broad picture of various categories of less than full-time, full-year employment experience, against the background of full-time, full-year employment, serves to emphasize that such employment experience, although in sum accounting for a very large part of the total, is in fact highly concentrated in certain demographic groups. But another point deserves emphasis. The rates of part-time and intermittent employment for the adult white male worker, particularly in the central age groups 35–44 and 45–54, are so low as to suggest that they offer very negligible cause for concern. It might even be hazarded that these rates are too low, in the sense of really not offering adequate expression of needs on the part of some workers in these age groups to have other than full-time work experience. In other words, the pressures to conform to the dominant white male adult work patterns, involving, among other things, full-time, full-year work experience, may be so great as to involve rather high psychic costs to an (unknown) fraction of the white adult male work force who would prefer to work less rigid schedules but are either afraid to or are not given real options to work a more flexible schedule. In any case it is clear that there is not very much underutilization of labor in this particular group.

But, on the other hand, the concentration of part-time employment experiences in other groups suggests that the very high rates in the case of some demographic categories may indeed represent very high personal cost and at the same time serious underutilization.

CHAPTER VII

SOME DIRECTIONS
FOR POLICY

THIS INVESTIGATION of the peripheral worker in America started from, and has centered upon, some of the implications for policy of what is a central social statistic of our time: the percentage of the population who come into contact with the world of work during the course of the year but whose relationship to work is different from that of the full-time, full-year worker. During the period in which work experience has been collected systematically, from 1950 to the present, approximately 45 percent of those who work during the year have consistently had less than full-time, full-year work experience. When unemployment rates fall, there is a slight decrease in this percentage. But even when unemployment rates go above 6 percent, the percentage of those with less than full-time, full-year employment does not rise by more than a point or two.

It is tempting to assume that there is something in the structure of the modern industrial economy which tends to make for comparative stability in the proportion of full-time, full-year workers to all those who have work experience during the course of the year. However, it was also tempting in the 1950s to assume that the percentage of those with part-time work experience would continue to increase, especially since part-time work experience seemed to be closely linked to participation of women in the labor force and labor force participation rates of women were increasing and were expected to increase in the future. But the percentage of those whose work experience is part time in fact leveled off just when predictions that it would probably increase for most of the decade of the 1960s began to be made. In fact, predictions about the probable size of the labor force over any extended period of time and of its components carry a great deal of uncertainty. A comparison of the projections made in the past by such careful investigators as Durand with the actual changes that have taken place in the size of components of the labor force impresses one with how rapidly projections based essentially upon extrapolations of trends can become obsolete.

Ideally policies designed to make it possible for peripheral workers to cope with the special problems which are connected with the character of their work experience should be based upon a fairly accurate estimate of the numbers of such peripheral workers at various points in the future when such policies are likely to take effect. Projections of this sort are doubly liable to be refuted by the future. The labor force participation rates of those demographic groups that make up the bulk of the peripheral labor force have themselves been much more variable than the labor force participation rates of adult white males. Moreover, this variability is the result of extremely complex economic and social circumstances. At the same time it is hazardous to predict what proportion of these very demographic groups will choose to, or be compelled to, work part time or intermittently.

Nevertheless, the projections of the size of the labor force as a whole and of the size of its major demographic components that have been made by the Bureau of Labor Statistics for 1970, 1975, and 1980 do indicate that the size of that portion of the population from which the peripheral labor force is currently drawn can be expected to increase while at the same time its components are changing their relative sizes. For each five-year period there is a markedly different pattern of percentage increases by age group, sex, and color. Over the entire fifteen-year period, 1965 to 1980, there is projected, however, a noticeable change in the character of the total labor force. It will, it is predicted, be younger, more female, and more nonwhite in composition. Indeed, the projected increases in nonwhite youth are of a very large order. On the other hand, for some of the older age groups there will be, it is anticipated, an absolute decrease in numbers, particularly for white males.

Although the passage of time may serve to make present alarms appear foolish, it seems the better part of wisdom to assume that there is some likelihood that the peripheral labor force will grow in size in the decades ahead and that, along with an increase in its size, old problems associated with some kinds of peripheral work experience will persist and become even more severe while new and unforeseeable problems will arise. Both the effect of new technology and the influence of shifts in consumer demand, particularly if they continue to be in the direction of a growth of the service sector at the expense of the other sectors of the economy, may raise serious questions of public policy, near the heart of which will be the circumstances of the peripheral worker and, more generally, the situation of the demographic groups from which he or she is presently drawn.

SOME POLICY IMPLICATIONS

What are some of the fundamental policy implications which emerge from an over-all consideration of peripheral work experience? Several seem to stand out. First of all, since peripheral work experience covers immensely broad and varied fields of human activity, it is essential that a general manpower policy take into account as thoroughly as possible the spill-over effects of any particular measure. To be more specific, a measure intended to stabilize work experience in general might have the unintended effect of drying up sources of peripheral work experience which are an essential element in the total lifetime work experience of individuals. Part-time or intermittent employment is a desirable option for many people, for teen-agers, for college students, for postgraduate students, for married women, for mothers with young children, for older workers, for individuals whose life style is not patterned around family and total commitment to work. A healthy economy should provide an adequate supply of peripheral work experience opportunities to match the demand for such work on the part of individuals whose circumstances differ from those of the typical full-time, full-year married male worker.

An attentive government will examine policies which do not seem to have a direct manpower purpose to see what impact they may have on the situation of peripheral workers. Urban renewal, for example, may inadvertently eliminate certain types of peripheral work experience which have traditionally provided essential income and constructive activity for some young people if renewal projects decrease the number of retail food shops and other firms which have provided after-school work to delivery boys. Changes in transportation patterns or increases in transportation costs may have a differentially large effect upon peripheral workers.

In any case it is likely that great urban centers will find it increasingly difficult, within their own geographical boundaries, to furnish the kind of peripheral work experience, particularly summer employment, which in the past has been part of the crucial process by means of which young persons explore the world of work and at the same time help to finance their education. At the other end of the age scale the great metropolis may be unable to furnish adequate amounts of peripheral work experience for older workers who desire part-time or part-year employment to supplement their retirement income or to ease the shock of an otherwise too abrupt retirement. The presence of large numbers of elderly individuals in the great cities, particularly women who have no family ties and very inadequate incomes, suggests that an increase in the opportunities for peripheral work experience for this group would be desirable.

Public policy, therefore, should be directed to maintaining and even enlarging the opportunities for peripheral work experience where this plays a constructive role in the life of an individual. In particular it is important that adequate opportunities for constructive peripheral work experience be provided for the teen-ager growing up in slum areas. Since it is very likely that such a young person does not ordinarily have adequate access to peripheral work experience within the boundaries of the urban slum, serious thought should be given to methods of providing such work experience for him, particularly during summer months.

In smaller communities and in the suburbs access to summer employment is apt to be through informal and personal relationships. There does not seem to be any obvious substitute available to the slum child for such supportive relationships to help introduce him to work. Perhaps schools can do more to develop programs and guidance in this area. It is possible, however, that summer and part-time work programs for the urban teen-ager should be kept quite separate from the school system because the slum child, particularly the school dropout, is apt to associate a work program carried out under the aegis of the schools with lack of success in school work and with a sense that school-related work experiences inevitably represent an artificial rather than a real experience with work. It is essential that programs which offer work experience to teen-agers who come from slum areas should be designed so as to lead to eventual full-time commitment to work. The worst possible result would be for the early employment experience of the slum teen-ager to confirm in him any developing feelings he may have that he is destined to repeat the casual and irregular employment experience of many of the adults in his environment.

Up to this point we have been emphasizing the importance of an adequate supply of constructive peripheral work experience for specific groups, particularly teen-agers, older workers, and mothers who desire to supplement their income with earnings from part-time work. But it is important to keep in mind that there is another side to peripheral work. The peripheral worker is concentrated very heavily in occupations which require little skill and he is often employed by small firms that offer little training to part-time or intermittent employees. Large, heavily capitalized firms generally employ full-time, full-year workers. Such large firms are more apt to be strongly unionized and to operate with very formal hiring and firing procedures. It is hard for workers with little education, little training, and a history of irregular and casual employment to surmount the barriers raised by these procedures.

Several important consequences follow from this general situation. A worker who is 30 years old and whose employment experience has been largely peripheral up to that age is quite possibly on a dead-end road as far as a work career is concerned. He is much less apt than a full-time, full-year worker to have received any training, much more apt to be a victim of seasonal ebbs and flows of production, much more apt to find himself superfluous in a recession, much more apt to be employed by small firms subject to wide variations in output and short lifetimes. He is much less protected by public policy designed to maintain income or shield him from the consequences of illness, accident, or old age. He is less often able to count upon a strong union to interpose itself between him and arbitrary and abrupt termination of employment. He is much more dependent upon casual sources for information about job opportunities.

Finally he is much more apt to withdraw from the labor force entirely if his work experience becomes increasingly peripheral. Although no definitive statistics are available upon which to base generalizations about the process by which a worker becomes increasingly uncommitted to work while he is still in the prime age group (25–54), it is clear that workers who have been full-time, full-year workers do not give up their commitment to work easily. It seems likely, however, that many of the recent migrants from the South to the great urban centers of the North, already highly peripheral in the work experience which follows their having been pushed off the land by technological change, may finally drop out of the labor market entirely if their work experience in the city falls below a minimum level. In the South, particularly in the smaller communities, they have been part of a labor pool which depended upon an informal network of information to provide its members with occasional work. In the large northern cities, these recent migrants may have no access to this kind of information and no experience in making use of more formal types of information about job opportunities.

What, then, can public and private policy do for those individuals, all too frequently nonwhite, all too frequently the most defenseless members of society because of age or marital status, whose peripheral work experience places them in such disadvantageous positions? Can anything be done to break the chain of circumstances which fastens casual and irregular employment upon those individuals whose lives are in many other respects also subject to great hazards?

Since peripheral work status is apt to be associated with low levels of skills, low educational attainment, and the absence of any significant amount of formal or on-the-job training, since it is associated frequently with low wage rates and even lower yearly income, manpower policies designed to improve the situation of the peripheral worker must be both broad in range and deep in effect. Like most specific manpower policies, successful action will depend in the last analysis upon the maintenance of very low rates of unemployment in the nation as a whole. Indeed, the problem of the peripheral worker does not really exist as a specific problem until low rates of unemployment in general are attained. It is only in such a tight labor market that it is possible to see clearly what groups in the population do not have access to sufficient peripheral work experience and to distinguish those groups who seem to be enmeshed in peripheral work experience unwillingly and at the cost of a fuller commitment to more productive work.

But assuming that the economy as a whole is able to maintain very high rates of employment, can we expect that the problems of the peripheral worker will disappear? Seen in this light, the problem of the peripheral worker becomes a specific aspect of the general problem of structural unemployment, a facet of the larger problem of ensuring that the supply of workers of all types, including those who wish partial rather than full employment for themselves, matches the demand for workers of all types.

The available evidence seems to indicate that high levels of employment in the country as a whole are not likely to alleviate to a tolerable extent the employment problems of the peripheral workers in the central cores of large cities. To some extent it may be possible for some nonwhite peripheral workers to relocate themselves in the suburbs where more stable employment opportunities may exist for them, but it is hardly likely that the flow of nonwhites out of the central cities can be sufficiently rapid to bring down the very high rates of peripheral employment in the ghetto areas.

If present rates of unemployment, underemployment, and

nonparticipation in the labor force of the nonwhite worker in the great city ghettoes continue much longer, they threaten to increase the sense of despair and the sense of alienation and demoralization to truly dangerous degrees. Rather than place all our trust in the long-run beneficent effects of high nation-wide employment rates on the situation of the nonwhite urban worker, it seems better to begin to plan and carry out programs to create more stable employment opportunities for the nonwhite urban worker *where he presently lives*. Public and private manpower policy might properly be directed toward locating those types of public and private enterprises whose employment practices are highly stable in areas where the peripheral worker now lives. It might prove more sensible in the long run to put as much effort and financial support into the provision of stable employment opportunities in slum areas as into public housing in those areas. It is of particular importance that workers who are trapped in a sequence of peripheral work experiences should finally be offered employment which contains a considerable component of on-the-job training to make up for their relative deprivation in this respect.

There are indications that powerful political and nonpolitical forces are beginning to feel that the solution to the employment problems of the great cities of America must include intensive efforts to establish public and private enterprises within the boundaries of slum areas. It seems certain that such efforts will succeed only if imaginative techniques of subsidy are developed. Powerful economic forces at the present time make the location of industrial and commercial activity in the central cities less and less attractive to private enterprise.

On the other hand, if the low productivity of many of the individuals in slum areas is due to a combination of inadequate education (it is almost a certainty that the Negro in a large city who is a recent migrant from rural southern areas is edu-

cationally deprived) and of inadequate opportunities to receive job training because of casual and irregular employment
experience, then there is a strong economic argument that sup-
ports temporary protection or subsidy of his employment in
industries and occupations which, by offering a large component of training, will increase his productivity and lead to
more stable work experience. But, as in the case of "infant
industry" tariffs, the problem of subsidized employment designed to lead to an increase in the productivity of workers
centers around the appropriate moment for the eventual removal of the subsidy. A successful subsidy program will lead
to increases in productivity, the gains of which accrue either
to the employer or to the employees themselves. The subsidy
should properly decrease as labor productivity increases until
finally the productivity of the workers has reached a point
where it is economically profitable to employ them in industries which provide stable employment at satisfactory unsubsidized wages.

It will not be easy, however, once a subsidized employment
program has been set in motion to persuade either employers
or employees to accept a reduction in subsidies. The more the
subsidy is relatively invisible, the more difficult will it be to
bring about its removal even when it is no longer justified. At
the same time there are real pressures upon political and business leaders to make subsidies take just such invisible forms—
tax abatement, writing down of land values, and so forth—
because of the public's deep-seated objections to direct wage
subsidies, which always seem to the man in the street to be
inequitable to unsubsidized workers.

Programs whose aim is to lead the peripheral worker from
irregular and low-paid work experience to more stable and
more productive employment should, however, by no means
be limited to the direct creation of jobs for such workers

through various types of subsidy programs. There are a number of other possible routes which can ease the transition of the peripheral worker to full-time, full-year status.

One of the most promising possibilities lies in the provision of fuller information to peripheral workers about stable employment opportunities. Because an individual is peripheral and therefore frequently lacks any direct personal contact with workers whose employment status is full time for the full year, because his educational background does not permit him to take advantage of the employment agencies which assume some degree of literacy, ordinary channels of information about developing job opportunities may pass him by completely. Just as the Census Bureau has found that it must develop new techniques of survey, much more searching, much more personal, and therefore much more expensive and more sophisticated, in order to establish even minimally adequate contact with the nonwhite male in slum areas, so employment agencies, public and private, must be induced to make much more direct, personal, and nonliterary approaches to such workers. The public employment agencies have traditionally not been fully satisfactory vehicles for providing employment opportunities. Meanwhile, private employment agencies have taken their cues very much from the employers to whom they refer job applicants.

If private employment agencies could look forward to some means of recouping the additional costs of providing information about stable employment opportunities to peripheral workers, their efforts to recruit such workers for full-time, full-year job opportunities could be expected to increase. Economists have recently recognized that there are frequently quite heavy "search" costs involved in locating a job. In the past these costs have largely been borne either by the employer or by the employee, or shared between them. "Search" costs for the peripheral worker trying to find full-time, full-year work are relatively heavy, and in his case the employer is usually not willing to pay an appreciable proportion of these costs.

For recent migrants from the rural South, public and private manpower policy must take into account the fact that many of these people, after having been displaced from the land, formed for a time part of a floating pool of casual labor which collected in the smaller towns and villages of the South. An active search for regular work in such communities was more or less fruitless. The employer simply went to wherever a pool of casual workers was to be found and chose as many workers as he needed. Such workers, transplanted to the northern cities, have little or no experience with the process of formal application for work and they frequently lack some or all of the elementary documents and work history that the personnel officers of large firms use as screening devices. For them, to seek work actively means to assemble each morning at the informal "shape-up" point. Since there is no real equivalent of this kind of labor market in the northern city, such individuals tend to drop out of the labor market entirely. Their work experience is limited, perhaps, to an occasional job of shoveling snow when the sanitation department is suddenly forced to recruit a large number of temporary workers.

Certainly one of the most important means to improve the employment status of the peripheral worker lies in a change in the practices of many personnel offices. Ivar Berg documents the inappropriateness of educational achievement as a screening device for many types of work.[1] So long as personnel offices, however, use a high school diploma as a screening device, many peripheral workers are condemned to the kind of casual employment by small-scale firms where a diploma is not required. The insurmountable barrier to employment that lack

[1] Ivar Berg, *Job Requirements in a Democratic Society* (Center for Urban Education, forthcoming).

of a high school diploma represents is a much heavier burden for the nonwhite peripheral worker. If he is a recent migrant from the rural South, the likelihood of a high school diploma is small indeed.

But it is not enough that personnel officers use realistic educational requirements. Another screening device is the work history of the applicant. The peripheral worker has, essentially, no work history from the point of view of many personnel officers. It is impossible for him to reconstruct his employment record. His work experience is so diverse, so full of gaps, that the ordinary employment application form is irrelevant. In addition to being unable to fill out satisfactorily the employment application, the peripheral worker frequently finds that he does not have many of the attributes of middle-class American life which increasingly are taken for granted by personnel offices and employment agencies. He does not possess a driver's license, he has no bank account. Moreover, his work history, if it is investigated at all, may include positive reasons for his rejection, such as a record of garnishment of wages or arrest.

Since the practices of personnel offices are designed to reduce the risk that any individual worker who is hired will prove to be an unsatisfactory choice, it might be possible to secure more flexible personnel policies if some of the costs of unsatisfactory employment decisions were borne, not by the firm, but by the public at large. Essentially part of the costs of personnel offices should be considered by the firm to be the equivalent of an insurance premium. Where the consequences and the risk of failure of proper performance are very large, the practice of bonding workers has already developed. Perhaps an analogous procedure could be extended to cover the type of applicant who at present seems to be too much of a risk for the personnel office of the average large-scale employer of blue-collar and lower-level white-collar workers.

Certainly it should be possible for public policy to devise ways by which the most obvious of barriers to employment, such as lack of a driver's license, could be surmounted. But where the obstacle to employment is a record of arrest or of garnishment of wages, both of which might indicate to the ordinary personnel officer a higher risk, public agencies might properly be asked to cover these risks.

The foregoing suggestions represent only a few of the possible ways of reducing the incidence of peripheral work experience where it is clearly an undesirable aspect of a person's work life. There is no claim that any of these suggestions is necessarily feasible, politically or otherwise. At the same time, it is almost certain that imagination and sympathy, coupled with a sense of the urgency of the problem and the need for bold innovation, can devise effective means of regularizing the employment experience of thousands of workers who at pres ent seem condemned to a casual and unsatisfactory relationship to the world of work. The revolution that has taken place within a few decades in the status of the longshoreman shows what can be achieved. But that same record indicates that a transformation in the status of the peripheral worker will not be costless, that it requires very careful planning, vigorous execution, and watchful concern for its long-term effects upon the total economy of the area.

Basically, public and private manpower policy for the peripheral worker should be flexible and specific at one and the same time. It should be based upon a clear understanding of which specific demographic groups are most severely subject to peripheral work experience. It should recognize that specific areas of the country, particularly the urban black ghettoes, suffer much more severely than does the country as a whole from the disadvantageous effects of undesirable peripheral work experience which are associated with high rates of unemployment in general and with unstable life patterns. Recognizing who is affected and where they are located provides the base for an attack on the problem.

At the same time it is just as important that public and private policy understand that peripheral work experience is highly desirable, indeed essential, for certain groups, particularly the young and the old, but also for other groups, such as women who need to supplement their income with part-time employment.

The problem of the peripheral worker in the nation as a whole and in the large city in particular is essentially one of matching the supply of workers with the demand so that to the maximum degree possible this matching does not lead to inequitable burdens being placed either in the short run or in the long run upon individuals and groups who are ill-prepared to cope with such burdens. Traditionally the peripheral worker in American society has been drawn to a large extent from immigrant groups. In the past many of these immigrants settled in the great cities of the nation where their children, if not they themselves, were able to make the transition from peripheral work status to the kind of well-paid stable employment experience which characterizes such a high proportion of white adult male American workers today. Some cities, pre-eminently New York, made very strong efforts to assist these earlier immigrants to make the transition from a low status in the world of work to a higher rank.

The stream of immigration into the large cities of the country today is no longer from foreign lands. It has in the recent past consisted instead of a vast flow of southern Negroes and Puerto Ricans into the same cities which earlier absorbed the immigrant from Europe and Asia. The challenge to the American city today is to make sure that as many of the adults who have made up this stream as possible become full-time, full-year workers and that opportunities are provided for their children to enter the same kind of occupations and industries which have made possible the enormous improvement in status and income that the white American worker has achieved in the past few decades.

On the one hand, the task is made immensely more difficult by the intransigent patterns of discrimination that surround the nonwhite worker, by the unconscionable delay in granting him elementary rights of access to education, residence, and employment, by the resulting accumulation of bitterness and the breakdown of communication. On the other hand, it is probable that this is the last time that the American city will be asked to absorb immigrants on anything like this scale. The effort, however costly it may be, needs in all probability to be made but once if it is successful. The immigrants to the great cities of America are already American citizens, most of them already know the language, they possess an immense reservoir of potential skills and energy which they themselves, as well as the country, need desperately to tap.

CONCLUSION

What has been said up to now has in an important sense been too general, too much a matter of percentages and categories. A more sensitive, a deeper way of examining this whole matter would call upon a very different kind of evidence. We are beginning to amass a body of material produced by the participant-observer, by studies in depth of critically important groups, such as those conducted by Robert Coles among Boston slum residents. A study of a very peripheral group of workers, the work of Elliot Liebow on the street-corner Negro, carried out in Washington, is a necessary complement to these remarks.[2] The informal shape-up of Negro men on a Washington street corner is one part of the reality behind the

---

[2] Elliot Liebow, *Tally's Corner: A Study of Negro Street-Corner Men* (Boston: Little, Brown & Company, 1968).

peripheral worker as we have used the term, and this type of labor market can be found in any city. It is far from a world of union contract, seniority, unemployment insurance, social security, and minimum wages. But so desperate is the situation of those who utilize this type of unregulated shape-up that they hope there will be no attempt to regulate it. To them, regulation of peripheral work of this type seems to threaten total exclusion from the world of work. To them, it is easier to move from peripheral work to no work at all than it is to move toward a stable employment experience. To them, the world of work has become completely bifurcated.

The question this book is concerned with is whether such bifurcation is a very general phenomenon. Do powerful, persuasive, though largely obscure barriers stand between the world of peripheral work and the status of full-time, full-year employment for many individuals? Do we take it for granted that peripheral work in general, and the most peripheral work in particular, should be performed by members of demographic groups whose status is lower than that of the adult white male group that provides the nucleus of the full-time, full-year work force? Will the full-time, full-year worker be increasingly found in those sectors of the economy where large-scale, bureaucratic, usually heavily capitalized firms are the rule? Do we make an overinvestment in human capital in those workers who possess full-time, full-year status and an underinvestment in human capital in peripheral workers? If so, does this in itself constitute one of the important barriers between the peripheral worker and employment in those sectors of the economy that can provide continuity of employment?

To some extent peripheral work experience is unquestionably a manifestation of increasing options available to many individuals. To the extent that it does represent an enlargement of the area of choice of work experience, it is a positive aspect of the economy. On the other hand, to the extent that the peripheral worker is treated as if he were a second-class worker, peripheral work experience cannot but lead to waste, frustration, and angry despair.

The peripheral worker in our society provides the economy with a very important part of the flexibility which it must have if it is to be efficient and dynamic. Recognizing this function, we should try to ensure that an undue share of the cost of this flexibility does not fall upon the peripheral workers themselves, many of whom are among the least able in our society to bear such costs. In the past, the immigrant provided much of the flexibility that a growing economy required and he often paid too much of the costs. We should ask ourselves today whether new groups have taken the immigrant's place. If the answer is "Yes" even in part, we should develop policies which will ensure that the costs of flexibility are not shifted onto the peripheral workers and in the long run this is much more important—that the social and economic barriers to movement from peripheral work status to full-time, full-year status are reduced to the point where we can truly affirm that part-time and intermittent work experience represents an enlargement of option and opportunity, not a contraction of life's possibilities.

INDEX